Life in Modern Britain

New Edition

Peter Bromhead

Emeritus Professor of Politics, University of Bristol

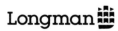

Longman Group UK Limited,
Longman House, Burnt Mill, Harlow,
Essex CM20 2JE, England
and Associated Companies throughout the world.

First published 1962
Seventh edition 1991

Set in 10/13 Plantin 113
by Servis Filmsetting Ltd, Manchester

Printed in Great Britain
by BPCC Hazell Books, Aylesbury

ISBN 0582 03642 9

Acknowledgements

We are grateful to the following for their permission to
reproduce copyright photographs:

Allsport / Bob Martin for page 191. Barnaby's Picture
Library for page 152 (top). John Birdsall Photography for
pages 90 and 162. Blackpool Tourism Department for page
98 (top). Britain on View for page 98 (bottom). Camera
Press, London for pages X (top) and 122 (bottom). Sally &
Richard Greenhill for pages X (bottom), 112 (bottom), 119,
129, 132 and 145 (top). Guildhall Press Office for page 63.
Hulton-Deutsch for page 30. National Trust Photographic
Library for page 7. Network / Martin Mayer for page 21, /
Mike Abrahams for pages 58 and 68, / Laurie Sparham for
page 122 (top) and / John Sturrock for page 139. Pacemaker
Press International for page 185 (top). Popperfoto for pages
12, 75 and 152 (bottom). Report / IFL Archive / John
Harris for page 78 (bottom). Rex Features for page 185
(bottom). Spectrum Colour Library for pages 174 and 179.
The Telegraph Colour Library for page 93. Topham Picture
Source for pages 48 and 188. UBS Phillips & Drew for page
78 (top). University of Sussex for page 145 (bottom). Zefa
Picture Library UK Limited for page 112 (top).

Cover photograph by Telegraph Colour Library Limited.

Picture research by Sandra Assersohn

Preface

There have been so many changes in economic, social and political life in Britain in the 1980s that this seventh edition is very different from the sixth (published in 1985). Some chapters have been completely rewritten, the others very thoroughly revised.

The book's purpose is to present a picture of the main aspects of the life of the British people in the last decade of the twentieth century. The emphasis is mainly on those features of British life which are distinctive or characteristic of Britain rather than of Western Europe as a whole. Past history is mentioned only where there is a need to show the background of today's developments.

The book assumes a good general knowledge of the English language, but includes explanations of terms like 'magistrate' or 'public school', which are used in special ways and may be unfamiliar to some readers. As far as possible the jargons used by bureaucrats and lawyers, social scientists and experts in business management, are avoided.

Most of the innovations of the 1980s have been controversial, many of them instigated by Mrs Thatcher's government. I have tried to show the nature of the changes and their purpose, but not to defend or criticise them. Both the text and the extended new statistical tables and figures at the ends of most chapters are intended to provide readers with material on which to base their opinions, and each chapter is followed by suggestions of topics for discussion, mainly in the form of questions: some broad, and some directed to particular problems. Most of the statistics have been extracted from official publications, in particular the 1989 edition of *Social Trends*, produced by the Government's statistical service.

For some of the ideas in this book I should like to thank my own colleagues and students in the Universities of Durham, Florida, Wales and Bristol, as well as the students and members of adult groups to whom I have lectured all over Europe, and in Sweden in particular. The Swedish summer schools have been very helpful to me in showing what aspects of the British scene produce points of difficulty for discussion, and I have been much helped too by students in other countries.

Contents

To Alison and Marjory-anne

A view of the Lake District.
Shoppers at a London street market.

1

The Country and the People

1 Stability and Change

For nine centuries the sea has protected the British from invasion and foreign occupation. During all this time the hereditary monarchy has survived, but with frequent changes to the limits on its power. There has been no political upheaval for 300 years, and the revolution of 1688 had no effect on the structure of society. It merely sent one king into exile, without violence, and replaced him by what may now be called a constitutional monarchy. The main institutions already established by that time were unaffected except by some fresh definition of their roles. Since then state power has been transferred by stages to a prime minister and government depending on a popularly elected parliament, in which it is usual for one party to have an overall majority of seats.

The British like to think that they excel in the qualities of moderation and tolerance. Such claims are obviously reinforced by the stability of government through several centuries without a written constitution and without clear definitions. These qualities demand self-discipline and mutual respect between people. Pedestrians cross streets against red lights when there are no cars coming, and nobody harasses them; but car drivers obey the lights and regularly respect the pedestrian crossings.

Since the 1960s the tolerance and moderation have been less evident than before, at least in politics and public life. For a long time until then, Conservative opinion had been ready to accept the advance towards equality. Governments of all parties maintained the welfare state, consulted the trade union leaders when forming economic policy, and imposed heavy taxes on the relatively rich. It was said that there was a 'consensus' giving high priority to personal security and the reduction of old class divisions.

By the 1970s it was evident that Britain's achievements, as an industrial economy, had been poor. Britain had once been the most productive and prosperous country in Europe. Now it had been overtaken by all the others of north-western Europe.

On the one side this national failure was ignored, or attributed to the survival of the capitalist economic system. There was impatience with the rate of social progress, resentment that inequality survived. All established authority was criticised and questioned, except that of the trade union leaders whose authority was respected because they pursued the interests of the working class.

On the other side it was thought that Britain had suffered from too much security, too little reward for enterprise, too much action by the state to protect inefficient industries and businesses.

The two attitudes could not be reconciled.

When the people voted to choose a government in 1979, they put the Conservatives in power. Under Mrs Thatcher's leadership they reversed the trends of the previous decades. They soon took measures to reduce trade union power. They revived the free enterprise capitalist economy, with its risks, its competition, its rewards for the winners, its harsh economic penalties and lack of sympathy for the losers. From the mid-1980s, they sold off nationalised industries to the private sector.

Under this regime the economy improved. Most denationalised industries made profits, to the benefit of the people who bought shares in them (including many of their own workers). The proportion of people without work doubled in five years, but soon the productivity of those still working rose at a faster rate than in any other Western country. Then unemployment fell, until by 1988 it was below 10 per cent – still very high, but below the European average. In 1983, and again in 1987, general elections confirmed Mrs Thatcher's Conservatives in power.

At least two-thirds of the people felt that they were sharing in the new prosperity, with their cars and foreign holidays and comfortable homes. The majority, who had owned their homes for several years, could see the market value of their homes increase beyond their most optimistic expectations. They did not much resent the even bigger share in prosperity obtained by accountants, lawyers, managers of money and of advertising businesses. They did not much complain that many businesses ensured the high productivity of their workers by employing fewer people than were needed.

In order to cut taxes the Government used new methods to restrict expenditure for social purposes and the health service. It spent little on the roads and sewage systems. It cut the railways' subsidy. It was slow to impose and enforce rules to reduce pollution or to promote safety. It took new powers to oblige local councils to set limits to their expenditure – and to the local taxes.

Many of these measures were not popular. Opinion polls showed that most people favoured better public services, and would accept the need to pay for them through taxes. All through the 1980s the Labour Party attacked the Government with increasing bitterness. This bitterness reflected the feelings of those people who became worse off under the new regime, or those who were angry at the growing gap between the rich and poor.

The tone of political argument in Parliament had already been more hostile in the 1970s than before, and became more hostile still in the 1980s. Many people in the country would have preferred more moderation, and there was a new surge of support for the Liberal Party and Social Democratic Party (SDP) which seemed to offer an alternative to the politics of confrontation.

The atmosphere of confrontation seemed to reflect a tendency towards belligerence in society as a whole. Hundreds of supporters of football teams, some of whom have made war on each other both inside football grounds and on the streets outside, brought shame to their country by their violence in Brussels and other European cities. There was violence too at some strikes, where hundreds of people gathered to prevent others from going to work. There were also violent demonstrations and other actions in support of various causes.

2 The Climate and the Regions

The British tendency to moderation perhaps reflects the climate, which is exceptionally moderate: not too hot or cold, not too wet or dry. The temperature rarely goes below $-5°C$ or over $25°C$. But the weather is often dull and damp with too little sunshine. The frequent moderate winds make it feel colder than it really is. July and August are sometimes fine, but more often miserable. There are no great differences of climate between the sections of the United Kingdom, except that the west has more rain than the east, and the northern mountains, particularly in Scotland, have much more rain and snow. More generally, the southern parts of England and Wales are a little warmer, sunnier and less misty than the rest.

Within England the eight administrative regions do not have strong cultural identities of their own. The styles of architecture do not vary, though there are parts of the south-west and north where stone houses were more common until recently than the red brick houses which predominate in most other regions. There is a clear difference between the northern way of speaking English and the southern way, though each has local variants and each is different from what has been called 'standard English' or 'received pronunciation', which has no regional basis and is spoken by about 3 per cent of the people, scattered around the country.

London's dominant position has been strengthened by the needs of modern times. For 100 years the central government has extended its responsibilities, partly by undertaking functions which were not performed at all before. With many local problems local representatives go to London to see central government officials. The main newspapers and publishers have their offices in London, so too do the advertisers and producers of television programmes. Like France England suffers, as compared with Germany, Italy and Spain, from excessive concentration of cultural life as well as business in a giant capital.

London has changed a great deal in the past fifty years, and is now perhaps more tolerant and easygoing than it used to be, with its society less consciously stratified. Far fewer people live in its central areas than fifty years ago; the old East End had 600,000 people in 1921, but has only 200,000 now. The air is now polluted more by petrol fumes than by smoke. There are no longer any of the yellow-black winter fogs that once shut out the sun.

A large proportion of the more prosperous city workers now live in distant suburbs, but there are a few rather small fashionable residential districts in the West End of London – though Mayfair, south of Oxford Street, now mostly consists of offices. Many districts, even near the centre, have a small-town life of their own, and some are dominated by people of a particular national origin – though not necessarily for more than a generation. The son of an East European Jewish immigrant of ninety years ago, leaving his comfortable suburb to visit his East End childhood home, found the old Yiddish notices gone, replaced by signs in Bengali. So much impermanence, change and movement have made the people more innovative, the place more lively, so full of surprises that nothing is surprising. The million or so new inhabitants from the West Indies, Africa and Asia have contributed much to the new atmosphere. The umbrellas and bowler hats of the staid old London are rarely to be seen, and they do not own the place any more.

From one generation to the next, London and Paris seem to have changed places. There are still more French restaurants in London than English restaurants in Paris; but London is richer in variety because people from every corner of the world run its restaurants. Before the 1950s a Londoner could well compare the slow, smelly, dirty Paris Metro unfavourably with London's Underground; today the comparison is the other way round.

In summer, London is now full of foreign visitors. Collectively they spend as many nights there as in all the rest of Britain, but those who see London as though it were the whole country are mistaken.

Outside London the southern half of England had for a long time more people than the rest of Britain. But from about 1800 the industrial revolution brought enormous development to the English north and midlands, to the Clyde estuary in Scotland and to South Wales. These were the areas rich in the coal to power the machines in the factories, and there was wool from the sheep on the nearby hills. By 1850 Manchester was a major industrial and commercial centre, with cotton mills mainly in the towns around it. The workers worked for long hours for little pay and lived in long rows of small red brick houses in insanitary conditions. The mill owners and their families prospered. Friedrich Engels was one of these, and his observation of the cruelties of this primitive stage of capitalism were reflected by his collaborator Karl Marx, then working in London in the British Museum library.

When people speak of the industrial north they think mainly of Lancashire and Yorkshire. Between the great port of Liverpool in the west and the smaller port of Hull in the east, the big cities of Manchester, Sheffield, Leeds and Bradford, along with some twenty big factory towns and many smaller ones, form a great industrial belt. Some of the buildings there are still black from smoke, some have been cleaned, and some demolished. Outside the towns the farmland is interrupted by coalmining villages, some still working. But many of the mines have been closed, their heaps of spoil grassed over, the winding gear still derelict or cleared away, replaced by modern factories. Further to the north-east, Newcastle upon Tyne is the centre of another industrial area (similar to Glasgow's in Scotland), which is based on coal, iron, steel and shipbuilding. The recent decline or rationalisation of the old industries, and the growth of some new ones, have brought new social life to city waterfronts.

But more than half the northern land area is sheep country, where the bleak moors of the Pennines have fine scenery and the valleys have picturesque villages. Many of the shepherds' cottages and village houses are now holiday and weekend homes for the people of the towns.

Not far to the south of Lancashire, Birmingham is the centre of the West Midlands conurbation. This is as big as Manchester's and has a vast variety of industries, particularly engineering. All through the east midlands there are other manufacturing towns, big and small, as well as coalmines.

Half of England's people live north of a line drawn from the south edge of Birmingham to the Wash. Four-fifths of them are in big towns or their suburbs.

Apart from London, the south has fewer big towns and far fewer smokestack industries than the north. Except for quite small moorlands it has almost no hills too high for cultivation. Most of it is undulating country with hundreds of small old market towns. The scenery is green and pleasant, but not spectacular.

With its lack of heavy industry and its slightly sunnier and milder climate the south is more agreeable to some people than the north, though it has less good scenery. In the past fifty years its relative advantages have grown. Being nearer both to London and to the Continent it has had easier connections with the outside world, and nearly all today's visitors from other continents arrive at London airports. The south's economy has adapted itself more easily than the north's to the needs of the late twentieth century, and it is the main base of the most modern industries and enterprises. More people stay at school after the age of sixteen, more go to university, fewer are unemployed, more have middle-class jobs. More have cars, more own their own homes and more have central heating (although the weather is less cold). Health is better: fewer people die of bronchitis or of other illnesses associated with poor living conditions, pollution or bad diet. Fewer vote for the Labour Party. It is sometimes said that there are two nations, north and south, with a growing division between the two.

3 The Nation's Heritage

Much of what is most pleasing in England has been left to us by preindustrial society, or by the expenditure in the countryside of the profits made by the industry of the towns. England in particular has a very rich architectural heritage. Many of the greatest of the cathedrals and other churches, built between 1100 and 1500, are in towns which have not become industrial centres and which have preserved their old character, so that the cathedrals themselves stand surrounded by expanses of grass and fine old private houses, in a setting not often equalled in continental Europe. The countryside is remarkable for the wonderful variety of shades of green in the fields and the trees – a delicacy and subtlety of colour not to be found in other places, and which reflects the lack of extremes in the climate. The streets of old market towns and country villages are pleasing and harmonious, with the half-timbered houses of the sixteenth century in parts of the south and midlands, the seventeenth-century stone of the Cotswold hills to the west of Oxford, and the

A country house, owned by the National Trust.

dignified town terraces of the eighteenth and early nineteenth centuries in many parts of the country. Some of the best examples of this period of English architecture are to be seen in bigger towns like Bristol, Bath and Brighton.

Several hundred great country houses still survive from the eighteenth century and earlier. Most of the biggest of these, with their old furniture and paintings, have become in effect museums, with their vast gardens open to the public. Some are still owned by the families who have inherited them; typically they keep a few rooms for their private use and cover the cost of maintenance with the help of the admission fees paid by thousands of visitors each year. Many other houses have been bought and kept alive by the National Trust, a non-state organisation founded in 1895 to preserve the best of the nation's heritage. The National Trust is financed partly by entrance fees paid by visitors to its houses, partly by gifts, legacies and the subscriptions of its two million members. It owns and preserves not only houses and their gardens, but vast areas of moorland and mountain and 600 kilometres of coastline, all of which are open to the public. It is the biggest conservation society in the world.

Since 1945 the state has designated ten areas of wild coast or mountain as National Parks, and thirty-three smaller, less remote sections of country as Areas of Outstanding Natural Beauty, with severe restrictions on new quarries, industry or house building; but little of this state activity would have been successful if it had not been based on a foundation established long before.

Britain has a great length of coastline, and no place is more than three hours from the sea by car – except during weekend traffic jams. Nineteenth-century prosperity produced, in Brighton, Bournemouth and Blackpool, three of Europe's biggest seaside-resort towns, along with a dozen others, each now with 50,000 to over 100,000 residents, many of them retired. In summer their beaches and amusements are crowded with day visitors. Some resorts were once thought to be 'fashionable'; such a notion would now seem inappropriate, even for Eastbourne or Torquay.

Away from the resort towns the best parts of the coast are now protected against any new building or development, and the glorious scenery of the cliffs, bays and coves of the south-west and South Wales has been made accessible by continuous public coastal footpaths. The paths are rough, and the few energetic people who walk along them can easily find solitude.

The Lake District, in the north-west, is commonly considered the most beautiful part of England. Everything is on a small scale, and the hills look higher than they really are. It seems that before the beginning of the romantic movement in the late eighteenth century people were little concerned with scenic beauty, but that period produced Wordsworth and the other Lake poets, inspired by the perfection of water, trees and heather-covered slopes.

Only fifty years ago – and for centuries before – British people were the world's most active tourists, though not many foreigners visited Britain. Since 1970 foreign visitors have, in some years, spent as much in Britain as British people spent abroad. Relative economic decline had not made the country miserable for visitors. Britain has not much brilliant cooking and no Alps, and the sea is rather cold; but there are good reasons for admiring the architecture and the scenery, and for enjoying the tolerance and friendliness of the people.

Questions

TABLE 1.1

Population and area, 1986					
	Population (millions)	Area 000 km²	Population density per 100 km²	Birth rate per 1,000	Cars per 1,000
England	47.0	130	36	13.9	338
Wales	2.8	21	12	13.7	313
Scotland	5.1	79	7	12.9	250
Northern Ireland	1.6	14	11	15.9	246
United Kingdom	56.9	244	23	13.3	323
France	55.4	547	11	14.1	386
West Germany	61.0	249	24	10.2	441
Italy	57.2	301	18	10.1	393
Netherlands	14.6	41	40	12.7	346
Belgium	9.9	31	31	11.9	343
Ireland	3.5	70	5	17.4	201
Spain	38.8	505	8	12.1	249

1 Discuss the relative population densities.
2 Is it valid to consider the number of cars per 1,000 people as an indicator of the living standard?
3 Is the relationship between the birthrates and car ownership fortuitous?

TABLE 1.2

Two nations? Population change in principal regions

Region	Population (millions)			Population increase/ decrease 1951–85		Main party seats in Parliament 1987	
	1951	1971	1985	millions	%	Con.	Lab.
*North	3.1	3.3	3.0	−0.1	−3	8	27
*North-west	6.4	6.7	6.3	−0.1	−1	34	36
*Yorks and Humber	4.5	4.8	4.9	+0.4	+9	21	33
*West Midlands	4.4	5.1	5.1	+0.7	+15	36	22
*Greater London	8.2	7.5	6.7	−1.5	−18	58	23
Rest of south and East Anglia	11.5	15.2	17.0	+5.5	+45	182	3
East Midlands	2.9	3.4	3.9	+1	+35	31	11
Wales	2.6	2.8	2.8	+0.2	+8	8	24
Scotland	5.2	5.2	5.1	−0.1	−2	10	50

The regions marked * include the biggest cities and conurbations with older industries.

Note how the people have moved back to the south, away from the nineteenth century's industrial regions, and note the correlation between population change and the amount of support for the Labour Party.

In April 1989 the Gallup Poll asked a sample of 1,000 people all over the
country if, in their opinion, certain aspects of behaviour had increased or
decreased in the last ten years. Here are some of the replies, in percentages.

TABLE 1.3

British people's opinions about the British

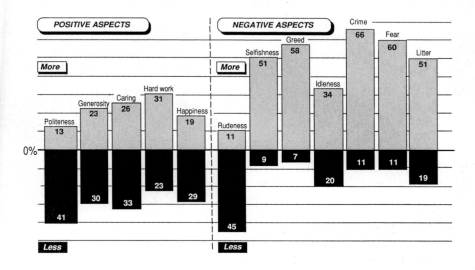

(Adapted from the Daily Telegraph, 29 April 1989.)

4 Do these figures illustrate any view about society? Or would you expect
similar results anywhere at any time?

Prime Minister John Major and his wife, Norma, outside 10 Downing Street.

2

Government and Politics

1   The Queen and the Constitution

Britain is a constitutional monarchy, without a written constitution. Some parts of the governmental system are written down in Acts of Parliament (also called 'laws' or 'statutes'), others are regulated by 'conventions', which are commonly accepted assumptions about the way things should be done, mostly based on precedents.

The present system has developed from the settlement which was the outcome of the Glorious Revolution of 1688–89. King James II had ruled for two years without a parliament, and had used powers which almost all sections of the people considered to be unjustified. By the end of 1688 he found himself deserted, even by his army, and he left for France, throwing the Great Seal of England into the River Thames on his way. An assembly of members of former parliaments declared the throne vacant, and offered it to King James's daughter Mary jointly with her husband William, who was also James's nephew. The army that he brought with him from Holland met no resistance. Instead, he was welcomed.

This revolution was accomplished without violence. The hereditary monarchy was preserved, but full sovereignty was placed in the hands of 'the King in Parliament'. The Act of Settlement (1701) and other statutes provided for a maximum interval between elections to the House of Commons (still on a very narrow franchise), and declared that new laws and taxes must be approved by Parliament and the monarch. But there was no formal restriction on the types of laws that might be passed. Any existing law could be replaced by another, provided that it passed through the prescribed processes.

The new King and Queen appointed ministers, at first without reference to Parliament. However, as time went on it became clear that the ministers could not work effectively unless they were approved of by the majority in the House of Commons. As that House consisted of two parties (Whigs and Tories), this came to mean that the ministers were all members of the party holding a majority of the seats (though the party divisions were for a time less rigid than they became later). The foundations of modern government were soon established.

At first there was no chief minister, but soon after 1721 Robert Walpole came to be called Prime Minister, and later it became normal for all ministers to be appointed on the Prime Minister's advice. The principle of the 'responsibility' of ministers to the House of Commons became well established, though this has always been difficult to define. In theory it has two aspects, in its modern form. First, the House of Commons may force any minister to resign. Second, because the ministers' responsibility is not only individual but collective, if the Commons force one minister to resign the others either disown him or resign as well. In practice individual ministers resign either because they themselves have decided to or because the Prime Minister asks them to. In either case the opinions of the Members of Parliament (MPs) of the party may have some influence, without being expressed by formal vote.

If a government is defeated on a vote of confidence, it does not need to resign at once. Instead, the Prime Minister may ask the monarch to dissolve Parliament for a new election. But any government with a clear majority of seats is unlikely to be defeated on a vote of confidence. Any MPs who vote no confidence in their own party's government have reason to fear that in a new general election they will lose their seats; so the supposed power of Parliament to remove a government has in fact become an instrument which helps the ministers, and the Prime Minister in particular, to maintain a rigid party discipline on all important issues. If a government has a solid party majority in the Commons it can normally feel secure in power until the next general election, which, by law, must be no more than five years after the one before.

As the system has developed, it gives almost unlimited power to a government whose party has an overall majority in the Commons. With no written constitution, any of the laws in force may be replaced by other laws, subject to the approval of the House of Commons and the monarch. Since 1949 the House of Lords has had no power except to delay the passing of a bill from one session of Parliament to the next; in practice this delay could be about three months. The need to get the Queen's approval seems to be a worthless safeguard, as she normally acts only as her ministers advise her. If she should ever think that she ought to reject her prime minister's advice, she would find no precedent for such action to guide her. It can be assumed that if she were to act alone, the government would resign, she would be unable to find other ministers acceptable to the majority in the House of Commons, and she would be obliged to call a general election. In that case she would be involved in party politics, and the whole status and position of the crown, as head of state and above party, would be destroyed.

In fact the existence of the monarch has until now provided some of the protection that a written constitution might provide against the improper use of governmental power. It is one of the most deeply respected of the rules or conventions of the unwritten constitution that the monarch should never be advised to act in a way which would seem to contravene the basis of the constitution, and so become involved in the controversies of politics.

2   The Government

The modern government is arranged in about fifteen departments, each with its ministerial head, normally entitled, for example, 'Secretary of State for Social Services'. The number of departments changes from time to time, as they are split or joined together. Normally, all the heads of departments are members of the House of Commons, though sometimes one is in the House of Lords. Nearly every head of department has under him one, two or three 'ministers of state', and at a lower level one, two or three 'parliamentary under-secretaries'. Altogether there are about fifty ministers of these lower ranks; about forty of them are MPs of the government's party, chosen by the Prime Minister for promotion from the 'back benches' of the House of Commons (which are used by MPs not holding ministerial offices) to join the government on the front bench. About ten others are members of the House of Lords.

The cabinet consists of the sixteen to twenty-four senior ministers whom the Prime Minister has appointed as members of it. These are the heads of the departments, together with a few others. The cabinet meets about once a week in Number 10 Downing Street, a rather ordinary-looking house which also contains the Prime Minister's personal office. He or she lives on the top floor. Number 10 is not really as small as it looks: there are big extensions behind the house, and the whole group of buildings is used by the Cabinet Secretariat as well as the Prime Minister's own civil service group and political officers.

There is no constitutional definition of the cabinet, which is in fact the politically active section of a much bigger and older institution, the Privy Council, which now has about 400 members. All cabinet ministers and judges in the Court of Appeal become members of the Privy Council for life, along with various other office holders and some individuals to whom membership is given as an honour. It still has some formal functions. Certain governmental decrees have to be promulgated by it, but each meeting consists of the Queen and any three members of the Council. Once three members were flown out to the royal yacht for this purpose. There is no discussion: just signing of prepared documents. When the Queen goes on a foreign tour another member of the royal family is appointed temporarily as her deputy in case an Order-in-Council is needed while she is away.

The cabinet makes the main decisions about government policy, as well as some others about which individual ministers disagree. Its agenda and proceedings are secret, though individual ministers sometimes give some indications to journalists about what has happened. There are many cabinet committees, some permanent and meeting regularly, others set up to deal with special problems. Each of these committees includes ministers from relevant departments. The Prime Minister decides who is to be in each committee, what each one has to do, and what matters are included in the full cabinet's agenda; he or she also has informal meetings with one or two ministers alone.

These arrangements are made necessary by the complexity of modern government, but they increase the Prime Minister's personal influence. This power is also helped by the Prime Minister's power to appoint all ministers, and to dismiss any of them at any time. Only one member of Mrs Thatcher's cabinet of 1979 was still there in September 1990 – and he then left too. Most had been dismissed or had resigned because of disagreements. Secretaries of state have so much to do in their own departments (not forgetting their work as MPs for their constituencies) that they cannot easily find time to think deeply about government policy as a whole. Because of this the Prime Minister is well placed to dominate the government. His or her position is strengthened by television, which tends to personalise politics; he or she is the effective equal of heads of foreign governments who are constitutionally more than first among equals; he or she has become party leader by defeating important rivals in a contest decided by the votes of parliamentary party colleagues.

Although they are commonly described collectively as 'ministers', nearly all the heads of departments have the official title of 'Secretary of State'. There were thirteen of them in 1991. The minister in charge of finance still has the archaic title 'Chancellor of the Exchequer', and the Lord Chancellor performs most of the functions appropriate to a minister of Justice. Several other archaic offices survive, but are now used for new purposes. The Lord President of the Council (i.e. the Privy Council) has in recent years been Leader of the House of Lords, and the Lord Privy

Seal has been Leader of the House of Commons; these two are in charge of the management of business in their respective Houses.

There are also other positions on the fringe of the government, held by MPs or peers. Two MPs of the party in power are appointed Law Officers for England, two for Scotland; then there are Whips in both Houses, concerned with the organisation of the timetable of business in Parliament, as well as with the maintenance of party solidarity. The table below shows these political offices as they were in January 1991.

	MPs	Lords	TOTAL
Members of the cabinet	20	2	22
Other ministers/Ministers of State	23	5	29
Law Officers	3	1	4
Junior ministers (Parliamentary Under-Secretaries)	24	6	30
Whips	14	7	21
TOTAL	84	22	107

Thus we see that, out of the usual number of 330–400 MPs of the party in power, about eighty hold some actual office. All these share in the whole government's responsibility.

No minister of any rank is allowed to indicate disagreement with any aspect of settled government policy, either in Parliament or on any public platform outside. If even a junior minister should criticise government policy, even in reply to a question from a member of the public during a political meeting in a schoolroom far from London on a Friday evening, the local press will report his indiscretion, the Opposition will hear of it, and in the next week the Prime Minister will have to answer an embarrassing question in the House of Commons. If any minister disagrees with any aspect of the Government's policy he must hide his disagreement and give loyal support. A policy which has been settled without a minister's knowledge, at a meeting where he was not present, is binding on him because he shares the whole Government's responsibility for policy. If he will not accept his share of that responsibility he must resign.

The requirement of ministerial solidarity does not extend to matters about which the Government's policy is to leave the decision to a free vote of the House of Commons, with each individual MP voting according to his own preference. Until recently such exceptions were rare, except in matters commonly seen to involve personal conscience or religious sentiment.

A minister who resigns through disagreement with the Government's policy may give reasons, and thereafter criticise his colleagues from the parliamentary back benches. Resignation often ends a person's career as a leading politician, but not in every case. Prime Ministers Eden, Macmillan and Wilson had all resigned office early in their careers and later come back with reputations strengthened; but each resigned for reasons in accord with party purity and in protest against compromise. It is probably more dangerous to resign on behalf of moderation than against it.

Her Majesty's Government is matched, or shadowed, by Her Majesty's Opposition; the informal arrangements assume a two-party system. The Leader of the Opposition is paid a special state salary, and appoints MPs and a few peers of his party to a 'shadow cabinet', as well as others as shadow ministers below the equivalent of cabinet rank. The main task of the shadow ministers is to criticise the Government. They are assumed to agree with all opposition policies and expected to support them, or otherwise to resign and return to the back benches. When the Labour Party forms the Opposition its shadow ministers are mostly elected by the party's MPs for the duration of an annual session of Parliament, but the Leader allocates the people to their departmental jobs.

Shadow ministers are helped by their party organisations and research staffs, but the ministers in office are more substantially equipped, each with a whole hierarchy of civil servants.

3　The Civil Service

When we speak of 'the Government' we tend to think of the ministers, who are politicians. But each department has a large staff of professional civil servants who do most of the work of running the department on the minister's behalf.

The Civil Service is wholly non-political. Those of its members who are in any way concerned with administration are forbidden to be candidates for Parliament or to give public support to any political party, though they may vote at elections. When a new government comes into office the same civil servants must work for the new ministers, who a few weeks before led the attack on the old ministers' policies.

In the three weeks before a general election, when ministers, as leading party politicians, are away campaigning for their party, the civil servants maintain the continuity of the administration of their departments. But they have also to prepare themselves for the possibility of a change of government, so they study the election manifesto of the opposition party, so as to be prepared to advise new ministers on the implementation of their programme if the election results in a change of government.

The Civil Service is a life's career. Most of those who advise ministers have joined the service after taking bachelors' degrees at universities, at the age of about twenty-two, though some have joined at an earlier age without going to university, and made their way up by promotion. Entry to the Service is controlled by the Civil Service Commission. People who hope to become civil servants must pass through a long selection process, with a series of tests designed to measure their competence and suitability, and many of those who are chosen have been among the most successful students in their university examinations. They are trained at the Civil Service College which provides courses both for newly-appointed officials and for those at later stages of their careers.

A civil servant in an established post has almost complete security of tenure, and can in practice only be removed for improper conduct. Promotion is not automatic according to seniority, but selective, and based on the recommendation of superior officers. A civil servant does not necessarily remain in the same department all through a long career; in fact when a department has a vacancy in one of its top posts it is very likely that it will be filled by someone brought in from another department. The chief official of a department is the permanent secretary, and below him are under-secretaries, assistant secretaries and others in a hierarchy. The permanent secretary is in close touch with the minister, and has the task of issuing directives which will put the minister's policies into force. Each civil servant must know exactly how far his personal responsibility extends, and what questions he ought to refer to someone higher up.

Many people say that Britain is really managed by the Civil Service, and that the ministers, being mere amateurs, just do what the civil servants tell them to do – or find themselves frustrated whenever they try to implement any new ideas. One of the main professional duties of civil servants is to shield their ministers from criticism in the House of Commons. Any innovation is likely to upset some established interest, which can be relied upon to feed some MP with material to attack it.

Genuine loyalty to the minister in office is the first element in the professionalism of any civil servant, skill in defending departmental positions is the second; and an ability to seem to reconcile the two, even when they conflict, demands intelligence, hard work and flexibility. A successful civil servant is rewarded by high pay, state honours and a right to an inflation-proof pension at sixty.

Is there, then, a danger that the privileged civil servants may be prejudiced against the Labour Party's claimed defence and championship of the underprivileged? Many Labour ministers have paid tribute to the support which they received from their officials, though recently a few have dissented. Labour ministers in office in 1964–70 and 1974–79 appointed increasing numbers of their own party political advisers to supplement their civil servants, and Conservative ministers, in their turn, have done the same, but on a smaller scale.

4 Elections
a) The Rules

The foundations of the electoral system were laid in the Middle Ages. Since then numerous Acts of Parliament have modified the system, but never in a systematic way. Fundamentally the system still has its ancient form, with each community electing its (now) one representative to serve as its Member of Parliament until the next general election. If an MP dies or resigns his seat, a by-election is held to replace him. Any British subject can be nominated as a candidate for any seat on payment of a deposit of £500, though peers and Church of England clergymen are disqualified from sitting in the House of Commons. There is no need to live in the area or to have any personal connection with it, and less than half of the candidates are in fact local residents. There are usually more than two candidates for each seat, but the one who receives most votes is elected. A large proportion are elected with less than half of the votes cast.

The franchise (right to vote) became universal for men by stages in the nineteenth century; hence the rise of the Labour Party. Women's suffrage came in two stages (1918 and 1928), and in 1970 the minimum voting age was reduced to eighteen. Voting is not compulsory, but in the autumn of each year every householder is obliged by law to enter on the register of electors the name of every resident who is over seventeen and a UK citizen. Much work is done to ensure that the register is complete and accurate, and each register is valid for one year beginning towards the end of February. People who are just too young to vote are included in the list, so that they may vote at any election which may be held after their eighteenth birthdays. It is only possible to vote at the polling station appropriate to one's address. Anyone who expects to be unable to vote there may apply in advance to be allowed to send the vote by post.

In 1974–83 there were 635 MPs for the UK, each representing one 'constituency'; in 1983 the number was increased to 650. Because some areas increase in population while others decline, the electoral map, or division of the whole country into constituencies, has to be changed from time to time so as to prevent gross inequalities of representation. The

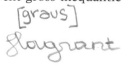

A candidate for election goes out campaigning.

citizen : [SITIZN]
resident : [rezidnt]

maximum interval between 'redistributions' is set by law at fifteen years – each time subject to Parliament's approval.

b) How Elections Work

The most important effect of the electoral system, with each seat won by the candidate with most votes, has been to sustain the dominance of two main rival parties, and only two. One forms the Government, the other the Opposition, hoping to change places after the next general election. The Prime Minister can choose the date of an election, with only three or four weeks' notice, at any time that seems favourable, up to five years after the last. At an election the people choose 'a Parliament' for five years and no more; but only one 'Parliament', so defined, has lasted its full five years since 1945. The shortest, elected in February 1974, was dissolved seven months later. The development of opinion polls gives the Prime Minister a good idea of his or her party's chances, month by month.

Until 1918 the Conservatives (Tories) and Liberals (formerly Whigs) took turns at holding power, then Conservatives and Labour. The Labour Party, formed in 1900 in alliance with the Liberals, replaced them as the second major party after 1918. Labour's success was made possible by divisions among the Liberals.

Between 1945 and 1987 there were thirteen general elections. No party ever received as many as half of the votes cast, but twelve of the elections gave an overall majority of seats to Labour (5) or Conservative (7); the winning party's percentage of the votes varied from thirty-nine per cent to forty-nine per cent. The exception was in February 1974 when the biggest party in the House of Commons, Labour, had only 301 seats out of 635. A minority Labour government took power. After only seven months Prime Minister Wilson called a second election, in the hope of obtaining an overall majority. With Labour winning 319 seats he just succeeded, though Labour had less than two-fifths of the votes. Within two years Labour had lost five seats at by-elections, but stayed in office as a minority government through an agreement with the Liberals. This was not a coalition, but the only period since 1931 in which a governing party relied on the support of another to remain in power.

This two-year period of minority rule was difficult for the Labour government, but Mr Callaghan, who had by then succeeded Mr Wilson as Prime Minister, could see from the opinion polls and occasional by-elections that Labour would probably lose any new general election if he used his right to dissolve Parliament. In March 1979 he was obliged to do so, at a time which he had not chosen, because his Government was

22

defeated by one vote on a <u>vote of confidence</u>.

The election which followed gave Mrs Thatcher's Conservatives a majority of 45 over all other parties combined. The Liberals had only eleven seats, the Scottish Nationalists three, the Welsh one. The two-party system seemed restored to its normal form, at least in terms of seats in the House of Commons. Mrs Thatcher called the next elections at four-yearly intervals, and won them both easily.

Although the Parliaments of 1979, 1983 and 1987 were dominated by a government faced by a big opposition party, with a few seats held by minor parties, a study of the figures shows how this <u>pattern</u> did not at all reflect the people's votes. The electoral system caused dramatic distortions, most particularly in 1983. By then the Liberals had formed an alliance with a new centre party, the Social Democratic Party (SDP). This alliance won almost as many votes as Labour, but Labour won almost ten times as many seats. The figures for the south of England were even more remarkable. In this area, covering nearly half of England's population, the Alliance's candidates (Liberals and Social Democrats) received almost 50 per cent more votes than Labour, but won only seven seats to Labour's twenty-nine. Labour's support was concentrated in parts of London, where it won some of its seats with big majorities. Outside London and the few big towns most Alliance candidates won at least twice as many votes as Labour.

The 1987 election produced results not greatly different from those of 1983, though Labour's share of the UK vote rose from 27.6 to 30.8 per cent, and the Alliance's share fell from 25.4 to 22.6. Labour's seats increased from 209 to 229, the Alliance's dropped from 23 to 22. Labour's biggest gains, in terms of votes, were in the big towns of Scotland and the north, in places with above average unemployment, in seats which they had already won in 1983.

Although Labour's small gain in votes between 1983 and 1987 was about equal to the Alliance's loss, it was not accounted for simply by people changing votes from Alliance to Labour. The <u>shifts</u> were in fact very complex, with big variations between constituencies. But overall the pattern established in 1983 survived, with almost a two-party parliament, and a government party holding a hundred more seats than all the rest together on the basis of a minority of votes.

The allied centre parties may have become the main alternative to the Conservatives in the south in the 1980s, but their achievement was made useless by the electoral system. Their supporters were too widely spread, mainly in areas where the Conservatives were stronger; so they won few seats. Labour's support is concentrated in areas where the party can win

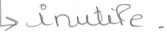

inutile.

seats; it does Labour no harm if it is the third party instead of being second, in terms of votes, in areas where the Conservatives are sure to win in any case.

The two-party system which is the essential feature of modern British government is a product of the electoral system, rather than a reflection of the wishes of the people. Many opinion polls, over many years, have indicated that most of the British people would prefer to use their most fundamental right, that of voting, in a system which would give fair representation. But both Conservatives and Labour claim that the existing electoral system is better than any other, and have produced objective arguments for it and the two-party dominance which it sustains. First, all the people of each constituency have one MP to represent them and their interests. Second, the system gives the people a clear choice between two alternative sets of leaders and policies. Third, it gives stable government for up to five years at a time. Fourth, because any person with realistic political ambitions must join one of the two main parties, each party includes a wide range of attitudes. Therefore, fifth, each party's programme, being a compromise, is likely to avoid extremes – and a government knows that within five years of taking power it must again face the judgment of the voters.

On the other hand it is pointed out that two-party choice at an election may be no better than a choice between two evils. Ministers of both parties, once in office, have developed a habit of claiming that at the last election the people voted to approve of every item in the winning party's election manifesto – although the truth is that only about two-fifths voted for the party, and many of these were more against the losers than for the winners. The claims about moderation, once well founded, have become less convincing in the past twenty years or so.

→ manifeste → pluriel manifestoes

5   The Parties

a) Conservatives

The Conservatives have always been the party of the Right, identified with the existing social order. The party's MPs alone elect their leader. Conservative values accept leadership in principle, and the party's leader is accepted as the director of its policies. When the party is in power its leader, as Prime Minister, chooses and dismisses ministers, moves them from one department to another, and expects their loyal support. When in Opposition it is the same with the Shadow Cabinet.

The party's Central Office is responsible to the leader. The MPs are expected to observe discipline and to vote with the party on several nights a week, usually at 10 p.m., and it is assumed that hope of promotion to ministerial office provides them with an incentive for obedience. But there is scope for an MP to try to influence the leader's policies by presenting arguments to Whips (and through them to ministers) and by speaking and seeking support at party MPs' specialist groups and at the MPs' weekly general meetings.

Outside Parliament the party has more than a million individual members who pay annual subscriptions, with an association for each constituency (reconstructed when constituency boundaries are changed). The most important function of an association is to choose the party's candidate for the next election, and then to keep in close touch with him as an MP if he is elected. The chief officers of the association have most influence; an MP who abstains or votes the wrong way in Parliament may be asked to explain that action to a general meeting of the association or of its executive committee, and the ultimate sanction is a decision to adopt another candidate at the next election.

When a constituency needs a new candidate, there are usually several dozens of applicants, some local people, some from other areas, most of them already on the national list of approved candidates. Two or three officers of the association may choose up to twenty of the aspirants for preliminary interviews, as though they were applicants for an ordinary job. Eventually, they reduce the list to about three or four to come before a full meeting of the association's executive committee, which has usually between 50 and 100 or more members. The committee hears the aspirants speak and answer questions, one by one, and then votes by exhaustive ballot until one is the winner.

The National Union of Conservative Associations is the partner, in London, of the Central Office, on which it may exert pressure. Each autumn a few representatives of each local association go, with the MPs and national leaders, to a four-day conference at a seaside town. There, with continuous television coverage, each section of the nation's business is debated for an hour or two, on the basis of a motion formed from several local proposals, and voted on, usually by a show of hands with a conclusion supportive of the national leadership.

Those who go to the conference are the most dedicated Tories. In 1975 the MPs chose in Mrs Thatcher the kind of leader favoured by the activists, and her radical policies have in general been well supported by the party as a whole. Tory purists welcome the privatisation of nationalised industries, the sale of council houses and the rhetoric of the state's withdrawal from direction of the economy. They also favour a strong stance on the pursuit of the national interest, and a high priority for defence and law and order. They would be critical of an MP showing weakness on these matters (they call it 'wetness').

Some of the MPs who promoted Michael Heseltine's candidature for the party leadership against Mrs Thatcher in 1990 were attacked for their 'disloyalty' by leading activists in the constituency parties.

b) Labour

The Labour Party's internal structure is in most ways like the Conservatives', but big differences arise from Labour's attempts to give much more real power to trade unions and ordinary members. Labour's annual conference is the supreme policy-making body of the party, and the parliamentary leaders are expected to follow its general policies when in power or in opposition. At each conference the unions and other sections of the party elect their twenty-eight representatives on the National Executive Committee (NEC) which makes decisions week by week. The NEC includes the leader and, usually, several ministers (when in power) or shadow ministers. Relations between the NEC and Labour cabinets in office have often produced bitter arguments, much publicised in the newspapers.

The form of the Labour Party's annual conference reflects the origins of the party as the political arm of the trade unions, when it was formed around 1900. With most of the unions most of the union members are affiliated through the union to the Labour Party. The union pays part of each member's subscription to the party, which derives most of its funds from this source. Each union sends a delegation to the party's annual conference, and at each vote its delegates usually vote together as a single 'block'. But the number of votes cast by a union depends on the number of its members who have been affiliated to the party. If there are 200,000 such members, the union casts 200,000 votes. But usually the union's vote is decided in advance by the small number of union officers who comprise its executive body.

As well as trade unions, the party also has other affiliated organisations, notably cooperative societies, which also send delegates to the conference.

People may also join their constituency Labour Parties, each of which sends its delegates to the annual conference, and each local delegation casts its votes, usually as a block, on the basis of decisions made at local party meetings. Figures for individual party membership are not published, but were estimated at about a million in the 1950s, 300,000 in the 1980s.

The votes at the conference are counted in millions, of which about one-sixth are cast by the constituency parties and nearly all the rest by union delegates. The system has been criticised, inside the party, as well

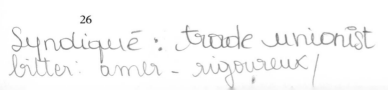

d'ailleurs → besides, moreover

as outside it, for giving a great deal of power to the few hundred members of the executives of the biggest unions, and it is possible that there will be changes in the 1990s.

In the period before 1983 the conference voted for withdrawal from Europe, massive new nationalisations and other left-wing policies. It also prescribed new rules for choosing the party leader, with Labour MPs and constituency party delegations having 30 per cent of the voting weight each, and the unions 40 per cent.

la gauche

The new system was first used in 1983 when Neil Kinnock, a 41-year-old MP from the South Wales mining area, was chosen as leader. He had been considered to be a man on the left. But the proportion of votes won by Labour at the 1983 election (27.6) had been the lowest since 1922, and the left-wing policies were widely blamed for this disaster. Gradually, the left-wing policies were abandoned, until by 1989–90, even before the events of that period in Eastern Europe, Labour's policies became much closer to those of the Social Democratic parties in much of Western Europe. Instead of proposing to withdraw from the European Community, the Party was attacking Mrs Thatcher's isolationism.

c) The Centre

Before 1918 there had never been a centre party in British politics. The new Labour Party had grown up as a small ally of the Liberals, to their left. Between the wars, after a disastrous division of the Liberals, the Labour Party, by then independent, took its place as the main alternative to the Conservatives, and the decline of the Liberals as a centre party seemed complete after they split (for a second time) in 1931.

In the 1950s there were about six Liberal MPs, elected in remote regions of Great Britain, but in many areas the party ceased to have any effective existence. In the 1960s growing dislike of both major parties helped Liberals to win some by-elections, and these local successes inspired a vigorous revival. At the elections of 1974 Liberals received a fifth of the votes cast, though only a dozen MPs were elected. In 1977–78, when the Labour government lost its overall majority in the Commons, the Liberals gave support to the government, which consulted them in forming its policies. In the period of this 'Lib-Lab pact' support for the Liberals, as shown by opinion polls, declined to 5 per cent, but then rose again to between 10 and 15 per cent until 1981.

In 1981 a second centre party was created, the Social Democratic Party. It was inspired by Roy Jenkins, a former Labour moderate who earlier had held all the highest offices in Labour cabinets except that of Prime Minister. He had then left Parliament and served for four years as

President of the European Commission. On his return to British politics he was joined by three other former Labour cabinet ministers and twenty other Labour MPs in forming the new party, which claimed that, free from the influence of the trade unions and of the left wing, it was the true successor of the Labour Party under its former leadership of Attlee and Gaitskell. The new party was soon joined by many people, including academics, who had not previously been active in party politics.

The Social Democrats and Liberals quickly formed an alliance of the centre, and at the end of 1981 had much more public support, according to opinion polls, than either the Conservative Government or the Labour Opposition. The two parties prepared an agreed statement of their policy, and each constituency had one Alliance candidate for Parliament, either a Liberal or a Social Democrat. But there were many disagreements, between the two parties and among the Liberals. The nature of the alliance was not clear. Its apparent success in receiving almost as many votes as Labour at the 1983 election was frustrated by the electoral system. All but three of the original Social Democratic MPs were defeated, mainly by Labour candidates. The Liberals then had more seats in Parliament and more members in the country, while the Social Democrats had the only political leaders with experience of office.

After the 1983 election Jenkins was replaced as leader of the Social Democrats by the younger David Owen, another former Labour Foreign Secretary, who quickly dominated his own party but appeared to be uneasy with the Liberals. In the next four years the Alliance had many successes in elections to local councils and in by-elections for Parliament, but failed to make a sustained advance. After the general election of 1987, in which the Alliance did a little less well than in 1983, most members of both parties agreed that they should merge to form a single party, and the merger was accomplished. But David Owen, with a nucleus of personal supporters, stayed outside. Soon there were two centre parties, engaged in bitter rivalry, though by 1990 Dr Owen's faction had collapsed and the united party, now called SLDP (Social and Liberal Democrats), or Liberal Democrats, stayed as the only serious party of the centre.

It had many successes in elections to local councils, and even gained a seat in Parliament from the Conservatives at a by-election; but in 1990 it failed to increase its support above 10 per cent in nationwide opinion polls. There was a new wave of gains in 1991.

d) Other Parties

Britain's Green Party was slower to develop than the Greens in some other European countries. At the 1979 election there were fifty-three

Green candidates, and they had on average 1.5 per cent of the votes in the constituencies which they contested. In 1987 there were more than twice as many candidates, and their average vote was the same as eight years before. About eighty times as many people voted for candidates of the centre Alliance, which itself gave strong emphasis to environmental issues.

By 1989 the Green Party had attracted more people ready to work actively for it, and to give it money. At the election for the European Parliament it had candidates for all the seats in Great Britain and gained 14 per cent of the votes cast – more than twice as many as the two rival centre parties combined. A few of the most successful Green candidates, in the safe Conservative areas where the centre Alliance had previously been most strong, came second with almost a quarter of the votes. The other parties soon reacted to this shock by paying more attention to environmental issues, and electoral support for the Green Party, in by-elections and opinion polls, fell back to 2 or 3 per cent.

Until the late 1980s the Communist Party reflected the aims of the Communist Party of the Soviet Union. Two Communists were elected to the House of Commons in 1945, but none since then. At the 1987 election the party had candidates in nineteen constituencies, where their average share of the vote was 0.8 per cent. In 1990 the Party's congress decided to abandon the name Communist, and seemed doubtful whether it would continue to exist as a political party. Other left-wing parties, some of them Trotskyites, have been even less successful. However, Communists and members of other left-wing parties have held influential positions in some trade unions, and the left-wingers who operate within the Labour Party continued to try to promote their aims within it after its main leaders moved towards the centre in 1987–90.

On the extreme right wing the National Front's few candidates at elections have in general been little more successful than the Communists. At the general election of 1987, it did not even have any candidates. At the 1983 election the National Front had sixty candidates, supporting 'the repatriation of coloured immigrants and their descendants and dependants'. A rival right-wing party had fifty-three candidates. Together these received less than 1 per cent of the votes in the constituencies which they contested, and none got as many as 3 per cent. This electoral failure, the worst for twenty years, contributed to the decision to stay out of the contest in 1987.

Although the electoral system tends to favour the Labour and Conservative parties against smaller parties operating on a nationwide scale, it is less effective in squeezing out parties with strong local support

The House of Commons, seen from the public gallery: 1 Press gallery; 2 Speaker's chair; 3 Opposition front bench; 4 Government front bench; 5 Dispatch box; 6 Galleries for MPs; 7 Civil servants advising ministers; 8 Galleries for distinguished visitors, including peers.

in particular regions. The Scottish National Party and its Welsh equivalent usually succeed in winning a few seats in their countries; even when their overall support is low they have continuing strength in some outlying areas. These two parties will be discussed in the chapter on Wales and Scotland (see pp.176–8).

⟨6⟩ The Working of the House of Commons

The two Houses of Parliament, the Lords and the Commons, share the same building, the Palace of Westminster. The Lords occupy the southern end, the Commons the rest, which includes some hundreds of rooms, among which are the library, restaurants, committee rooms, and private or shared offices for MPs.

The Commons debating chamber is usually called 'the House'. It has seats for only about 370 of its total membership of 650. It is rectangular, with the Speaker's chair at one end, and with five straight rows of benches (divided by a gangway) running down one side along its whole length, and five rows on the other side, so that the rows of benches face each other across the floor. One side of the House is occupied by the Government and the MPs who support it, the other, facing them, by Her Majesty's Opposition – all the MPs who are opposed to the Government of the day and who hope that at the next general election their party will be in a majority so that they can form the Government. The arrangement of the benches suggests a two-party system.

The front bench up to the gangway, nearest to the Speaker's right, is the Government front bench, where ministers sit. It has room for about seventeen people, but although there are more than sixty ministers (apart from whips) who are members of the House of Commons, this front bench is rarely full. Ministers do not usually sit listening to debates which do not concern their own departments.

Facing the Government front bench is the Opposition front bench, used by members of the shadow cabinet. There is a long table between the two front benches. Whatever the business under discussion, a minister from the department responsible occupies a seat near the far end of the Government front bench, faced across the table by an Opposition shadow-minister. Each of these seats has, on the table in front of it, a reading desk, called a 'dispatch box'. Ministers normally speak in Parliament only from the Dispatch Box, and only in their departmental capacity. What they say is said officially, and commits the Government as a whole – so they need a convenient desk for documents, including civil servants' briefing notes.

Members of the House of Commons have been paid salaries since 1911. The rate has lately been nearly twice the average industrial worker's wage. Since 1965 the allowances for travel, living in London, and paying part-time secretaries and research assistants, have all been improved. The library has been extended; its greatly increased staff help MPs to get the information they need for their work. But many MPs say that they need to have outside earnings, through journalism, work in the law courts or business, to enable them to live at the standard they expect.

Each chamber has galleries, parts of which are kept for the use of the public, who are described, in the language of Parliament, as 'strangers'. It is usually possible to get a seat in the Strangers' Gallery of the House of Lords at any time, but it is not so easy to get into the House of Commons Gallery, particularly in the summer, when London is full of visitors. In order to get a place for the beginning of a day's business at 2.30 p.m., in time for the question hour, it is usually necessary to write in advance to an MP for a ticket, though foreign visitors can sometimes get tickets through their embassies. A person who comes without a reservation usually has to wait for a long time, one, two or three hours, until a place becomes free, though very late in the evening it is often possible to get in without waiting. Television cameras were first admitted to the Chamber in 1989.

Standing Orders set out the main formal rules of procedure, but there are also practices established by custom and precedent. In 1844 Sir Thomas Erskine May, who was then Clerk of the House of Commons, published his *Treatise on the Law, Privileges, Proceedings and Usage of Parliament*. Revised editions of Erskine May have been published from time to time. It is used and followed in other parliaments of the Commonwealth besides the British. As anyone who reads it can quickly see, very many of the rules are derived from individual decisions of successive Speakers. A Speaker's decision on some particular point may establish a precedent in much the same way as a court's decision on a matter of law.

The choice of an MP as Speaker is made by a vote of the House after the party leaders have consulted their supporters and privately agreed beforehand on a particular person. A Speaker is customarily reappointed to his office in each new Parliament, even if the majority in the House has changed. Although first elected to Parliament as a party MP a Speaker must abandon party politics until retirement to the House of Lords. Three other Members hold office as deputy-speakers, and they take turns at occupying the Chair. The three deputies abstain from all party activity for so long as they hold office, but may – and sometimes do – return to ordinary political activity after a time.

The central rule of procedure is that every debate must relate to a specific proposal, or 'motion'. An MP moves (proposes) a motion; the House debates it and finally decides whether to agree or to disagree with it. A motion may propose that the House should take some action (for example, approve the principles of a proposed new law), or that it should express some opinion. When a motion has been moved, another MP may propose to 'amend' it, and in that case his proposal is debated. When the House has decided on the amendment it goes back to the original motion, which is now in a new form if an amendment to it has been accepted. A debate ends either (1) when every Member who wants to speak has done so, or (2) at a time fixed in advance either by informal agreement between the parties or by a vote of the House (that is, by the Government without the agreement of the Opposition), or (3) when the House, with the Speaker's consent, votes that it shall end.

At the end of every debate the Speaker asks the House to vote on the motion that has been debated. If there is disagreement, there is a 'division' and Members vote by walking through corridors called 'lobbies', being counted as they do so. The names of Members voting are recorded and published. The 'Aye' (yes) lobby runs down one side of the outside wall of the chamber, the 'No' lobby down the other side. Six minutes after the beginning of the division the doors leading into the lobbies are locked. The practice of allowing six minutes before Members must enter their lobbies gives enough time for them to come from any part of the Palace of Westminster. Bells ring all over the building to summon Members to the chamber to vote. Members often vote without having heard a debate, and even without knowing exactly what is the question; they know which way to vote because Whips (or party managers) of the parties stand outside the doors, and Members vote almost automatically with their parties.

Except in holiday periods the House of Commons meets every Monday, Tuesday, Wednesday and Thursday at 2.30 in the afternoon, and normally sits until 10.30 p.m., although it may continue to sit later still – often until eleven or twelve, and occasionally until one or two in the morning or even all through the night. On Fridays it meets at 9.30 in the morning and finishes at 3.30 p.m.

Many Members go to their constituencies, whether their homes are there or not, during the weekends. They need to see their local party organisers from time to time, and to be available to citizens who wish to discuss grievances or other problems. They also make speeches, not only in their constituencies but in other places too. On Sundays they can try to arrange things so that they can be with their families. But they also have holidays of about four weeks over Christmas, two weeks each at Easter and Whitsun, and about eleven weeks – from early August to mid-October – in the summer.

The life of Parliament is divided into periods called 'sessions'. At the end of every session Parliament is 'prorogued'; this means that all business which has not been completed is abandoned, and Parliament cannot meet again until it is formally summoned by the Queen. Every new session begins with a clean slate. A session normally lasts for about a year, from late October of one year to about the same date of the next year, though if a general election is held in the spring or summer the normal rhythm of the sessions is interrupted.

The beginning of a new session, called 'the State Opening of Parliament', is a fine ceremonial occasion, beginning with the royal carriage procession from Buckingham Palace to the Palace of Westminster. The Household Cavalry are there, also the Lord Great Chamberlain, Gold Stick in Waiting, the Master of the Horse, the Gentlemen at Arms, the Yeomen of the Guard and the Ladies of the Bedchamber, and of course the trumpeters, the crowds along the processional route, and now the television cameras. The ceremony takes place in the House of Lords, with leading members of the House of Commons standing crowded together at the end of the chamber opposite to the Throne, within the four walls of the room, but technically outside the 'House of Lords' itself.

The Queen takes her place on the throne and reads out the 'Queen's Speech', which is a document, about a thousand words in length, prepared by the Government, in which the Government gives a summary of the things which it intends to do during the session which is about to begin. The members of the House of Commons then go back to their own chamber, and a member of the Government party proposes that a humble address should be presented to the Queen to thank her for her gracious speech. A debate on this proposal then begins, and lasts for five or six days; it is really a succession of debates on particular aspects of the Government's policy as set out in the Queen's Speech. Usually the Opposition propose to add to the address to the Queen some expressions of regret about some part of the Speech or about some omissions from it; at the end of each debate there may be a vote on the Opposition's amendment. If the Government lost such a vote it would presumably have to resign or ask for a general election.

(7) The Parliamentary Day

Except on Fridays, each day's business begins, after prayers and some minor preliminaries which take about five minutes, with 'Question Time'. This is a period of about fifty-five minutes, ending at 3.30 p.m., during which Members may address questions to ministers, which ministers normally answer, although they are not obliged to do so. At 3.30 p.m. any minister may make a 'statement', and questions may be asked about it. Exciting but brief arguments often take place at this moment, and the House is usually rather full.

The other miscellaneous items which begin at 3.30 p.m. may take together no time at all, or ten minutes, or (more often) an hour or more. When they are finished, the main business of the day begins, and normally continues until 10 p.m., which under the Standing Orders is the hour at which the business should end; sometimes, however, the House has already decided at 3.30 p.m. to allow the main business to continue after 10 p.m. Then there are various special types of business which may be taken after 10 p.m., even under the Standing Orders; and finally, when everything else is finished, thirty minutes are allowed for any Member to

34

The Lord's prayer: l'oraison dominicale.
statement : exposé des faits, compte rendu.

make a speech on some subject and for the appropriate minister to reply.

The question hour at the beginning of each day's sitting is the most widely-known and admired procedural device of the British House of Commons, and it has been imitated – though not exactly – in many other countries. Two features of this procedure are mainly responsible for its usefulness and success: the use made of the supplementary question and the shortness of all the questions and answers. From thirty to fifty questions and up to a hundred supplementaries are asked and answered during the hour each day.

Every question must be handed to the officials of the House in writing at least forty-eight hours before the answer is to be given. The officials transmit the questions very quickly to the ministers who will have to answer them, and the answers are prepared by civil servants. For the sake of convenience, questions are not answered exactly in the order in which they have been asked. An informal rota of ministers is arranged, and each day two or three or more ministers deal in turn with the questions to themselves which have accumulated during the period – normally one or two weeks – since they last had their turns at answering. Thus on a typical day there may be eight questions for the minister who is first to answer, twenty for the second, and so on. The Prime Minister is outside the rota, and answers questions on general policy at 3.15 p.m. on two days a week.

All the questions for answer on a particular day are printed, together with the names of the interrogators, on the day's programme sheet (called the 'Order Paper'), and each question has a serial number. The Speaker begins the proceedings by calling out the name of the Member who is to ask the first question, and that Member simply stands and says 'Question No. 1'. The minister to whom it is addressed then reads out the reply (or, possibly, gives the reply without reading). Then the Member who asked the question may ask a 'supplementary' question asking for further clarification, and the minister is expected to reply at once to that also; he and his civil servants have tried to foresee all possible supplementaries, and to be ready with answers. Then other members may also ask further supplementary questions, and so on until the Speaker decides that it is time to go on to the next question on the paper. He does this by calling out the name of the Member who is to ask Question No. 2. The Speaker has to try to keep down the number of supplementaries enough to allow a reasonable number of questions to be dealt with, but not so much that ministers are excessively protected against awkward supplementaries. This is a difficult task.

It is not at all easy to classify or analyse parliamentary questions. Some are asked for the purpose of embarrassing the Government, some in order to try to persuade ministers to adopt new courses of action, either in dealing with individual cases or in their general policies. Everybody knows that if any official anywhere in the administration does anything stupid or harsh, it is quite likely that the person aggrieved will write to his Member of Parliament, who will first write or talk to the minister privately about the case, and then, if it seems that justice has not been done, ask a question in all the publicity of the House of Commons. So Question Time is not only interesting and a good opportunity for the display of skill and wit; it also helps in a very positive way to prevent the administrative machine from working without due humanity. There has been bitter acrimony at times, particularly with Prime Minister's questions.

If a Member is dissatisfied with a minister's answers, it is possible to try to raise the subject again, at greater length, by entering the ballot for the right to open the final half-hour 'debate on the adjournment' at the end of some future day's business. This gives time to develop complaints more thoroughly, but there will probably be only a few Members present. With very urgent and important matters there is a procedure which allows the planned order of business to be changed so as to allow about three hours to be spent on the next day in debating something that must be debated quickly if at all. But this procedure is used mainly by the official Opposition.

There are always more questions asked by members of the Opposition party than by supporters of the Government. Ministers do not address questions to their own colleagues, but it is commonly accepted that a member of the Government's party who does not hold any office ought not to hesitate to ask a question, even if it will be embarrassing to the minister, if there is good reason to ask it. In fact, there are always some Members on the Government benches who are readier to ask awkward questions than the majority of their colleagues. The House of Commons, like any group, always includes some personalities on both sides who are more forward than the average; it seems that in general some fifty or sixty Members together ask about half of all the questions, while 200 others hardly ever ask any at all.

After Question Time and the short items of business which sometimes follow it, the House of Commons goes on to the main debate of the day, to which it can usually give about six hours. Sometimes there are two or three short debates in succession, but usually one debate lasts for the whole of the time available.

In a normal twelve-month session the House of Commons sits for about 31–33 weeks. At the full-day sittings, Mondays to Thursdays, about five

the ballot: un tour (de scrutin)

or six hours up to 10 p.m. are spent on the main debates about the Government's policies – though about two or three of these days each month are opposition days, on which the official Opposition decides the subject of debate. (Three of these each session are given to minor parties.) Each Thursday the next week's programme is announced, and the parties give their members an indication of the times at which votes (divisions) are expected. This is done on a document called a 'whip', and a party's request for its members' support at a division may be underlined one, two or three times. A three-line whip signifies a vote of the greatest importance to the party.

The Government has final control over the timetable, and uses its power to ensure that during the session Parliament passes the bills which give authority to collect taxes and spend money, and the bills which give effect to the Government's own policies, as outlined in the Queen's Speech. The amount of time to be given to each item of business is decided at meetings of the parties' Chief Whips, in such a way as to balance the wishes of the two sides as effectively as possible.

A typical full-day debate lasts about five to six hours, with opening and closing speeches by ministers and shadow ministers speaking from their dispatch-box positions. If each of these four speeches takes half an hour, there are three or four hours between five or six and nine o'clock for fifteen to twenty backbenchers' speeches. The Speaker calls members to speak from the two sides alternately more or less at random, giving priority to Privy Councillors (and occasionally to a new Member for a first, or 'maiden' speech). In practice a Member who wants to speak may see the Speaker before the debate, and the Speaker may try to arrange the order of speeches so that as many different points of view as possible can be included.

The House of Commons spends about 1,500 hours a year in session; this is said to be longer than any other parliament. Towards the end of Question Time on most afternoons, the chamber is quite well filled, particularly on a day when an important or controversial ministerial statement is expected. But between six and nine o'clock there are often only twenty or thirty members to hear the backbenchers' speeches. Members spend most of their time at small group meetings, or talking with colleagues or people who have come in from their constituencies, or in the library, or in their offices answering letters or doing other paperwork, or away from Westminster altogether.

Whenever there is a 'whipped' division both major parties expect their people to vote. There is no provision for proxy voting or for recording abstentions. But except for three-line whip divisions (with the request to

37

vote underlined three times) it is quite usual for members of the two sides to be 'paired'; both agree to be absent, and register their agreement with the whips. For three-line whip divisions pairs are allowed only for very good reasons. Whenever there is a government in office with a small majority, as in 1964–66 and 1974–79, its party whips need to make sure that their supporters come in to vote. On a few occasions ministers cut short important foreign conferences, and MPs were brought in ambu-lances from hospital to vote. But in the 1980s there has been less pressure. Even so, if the balance of votes in a division indicates that members on one side or the other have been absent without pairs, there is embarrassment for the party with a shortfall.

In most weeks there are whipped divisions at ten o'clock or later on two or three nights. The names of the MPs voting are published in the stenographic record, which is called 'Hansard' because Thomas Hansard pioneered these reports in 1803, in defiance of a parliamentary rule. Now it is sold in government bookshops, so anyone can study the voting record of any MPs, and from time to time newspapers publish the names of those who have been most and least assiduous. The whips also have their own lists; so there is pressure on MPs, both from their parties and from the public, to be available to vote even at inconvenient times.

⑧ How Laws are Passed

The British Parliament, like parliaments in other countries, is often referred to as 'the legislature' – the body which makes laws. Its essential function could probably be best described as 'to discuss what the Government has done, is doing and intends to do, and on occasion to try to show up the Government's errors and to try to persuade the Government to change or modify its policies'. Nevertheless, new laws can only come into force when they have passed through Parliament, and the way in which it deals with bills (that is, proposals for new laws) gives a good illustration of Parliament's working.

Nearly all important bills are introduced by the Government. About fifty bills are passed each year, some short, some long, some uncontrover-sial, some needing much discussion. Every bill brought in by the Government has been approved first by the Cabinet in fact, in any year, there are nearly always more bills which the Government would like to have passed than it can find time to put through Parliament.

Once the Government has decided to introduce a bill, a minister is put in charge of it. The preparation of the text may take many months, with long consultations involving civil servants in the minister's department on the one hand and Parliamentary Counsel on the other. (These are a small group of legal experts who are concerned with the technical side of the drafting, or writing, of bills. All the laws in force are collected together in the 'book' of statutes, in which each law is a 'chapter'. Acts of Parliament have to be interpreted by the courts, and every law must conform to the special usages and interpretations of the statute book.) At the same time, the civil servants will probably have conferences with officials from other departments, and also with representatives of groups of people (such as associations of traders, manufacturers, workers, dentists, cyclists or people who keep bees) who may be affected or interested in some way by the proposed new law.

At last the bill is ready to be submitted to Parliament. It will have to be passed by both Houses of Parliament, one after the other. It can begin its journey in either the House of Commons or the House of Lords, though all really important or controversial bills are in fact submitted to the House of Commons first.

The typical bill of moderate importance, then, will begin in the House of Commons. According to very ancient practice, it must have three 'readings' there, although the use of this word is a little misleading. The 'first reading' is in effect merely an announcement that the bill is coming forward. After the text has been in circulation for a reasonable length of time (usually one or two weeks at least), a period of time, for example a whole day, is provided in the timetable of the House of Commons for the debate on the 'second reading'. This is the main debate on the general principles and objectives of the bill, and at the end of the debate a vote is taken; if the Opposition do not like it they will vote against it. A vote on the second reading of a Government bill is, like almost all votes in the House of Commons, an occasion when the members of the two main parties vote in blocks, with few deviations. The important thing about this stage is not the final decision, but the words spoken in the debate, the arguments for and against, the discussion of principles and of details from many points of view. A Government supporter may make a speech objecting to a bill or part of it, and then vote for it.

After a bill has passed its second reading, a 'standing committee' of up to forty-five MPs is set up to consider it in detail. (The very rare bills affecting the constitution have their details considered by the whole House, converted into a committee for the purpose). In any of these small committees, the parties have seats in the same proportion as in the whole House, so the government party normally has a majority. The seats in a committee are allocated by the Committee of Selection, a group of senior MPs who are supposed to be impartial but who may be influenced by party whips. For some bills too many MPs want committee seats, for others hardly anyone wants them, so that party whips can punish MPs who have given trouble by pushing them into committee jobs that they do not want. The ministerial chief of the department concerned, and/or one or more junior ministers, are always included as well as their Opposition 'shadows'.

Standing committees normally meet on two mornings a week in rooms off a long corridor on the upper floor of the Palace. The seats are arranged like a miniature House of Commons, with Government and Opposition facing each other, led from their front benches by ministers and shadow ministers.

A bill is printed in clauses divided into subsections, and committee members may propose changes to the text, one by one, in order. Whenever an amendment is proposed, the minister either agrees to accept it, refuses, or asks for it to be withdrawn so that there may be some private discussion about it. If he refuses, there may be a vote, but the minister's fellow party members usually vote so as to ensure a Government majority. Ministers do in fact very often accept proposals for amendment, either in their original form or in some form which is agreed to as a compromise.

Committee proceedings on a single bill may take two mornings a week for two to ten or even fifteen weeks, with dozens of proposals for amendment debated one after another. A debate may be closed by a majority vote if the chairman (who acts impartially) thinks the debate has been long enough. Long and controversial bills are usually 'guillotined', with a time limit for debate on each group of clauses.

The committee stage of a bill illustrates very clearly the position of organised groups of people who have particular interests in relation to the political process. Most proposals for amendments to a bill are suggested to committee members by associations which think that their interests are threatened, or not helped, by the bill as it has been brought in by the Government. They may have already presented their arguments to the minister or his civil servants privately beforehand, and their suggestions may then have been refused; in that case the committee discussion gives an opportunity to a Member of Parliament, acting as their spokesman, to oblige the minister to think again, perhaps to make a concession, or at least to make a public defence of his reasons for not giving them what they want.

After the committee has finished with a bill, the next stage is called 'the report stage'. The House itself now repeats the committee stage, though taking much less time. The House has before it the new text of the bill, incorporating the committee's amendments. Some new amendments are proposed and there may be further discussion of the amendments which were proposed in committee but withdrawn so as to give the minister time to examine them thoroughly. These amendments are now decided upon, or withdrawn again, pending further discussion in the House of Lords.

The last stage is the debate on the proposal to 'read the bill a third time'. This debate is usually fairly short. It is a final review and discussion of the bill as it stands after amendment.

Next the bill must go through the same stages in the House of Lords. If the House of Lords rejects a bill which has been passed by the Commons, the bill can go no further for a few months; but if the Commons pass it again, in substantially the same form as before, it must go to the Queen for her signature no matter what the Lords do. The position of the House of Lords is discussed on pages 50–53.

Normally, when a Government has an overall majority in the Commons, Parliament is not acting as a pure legislature, or law-making body, but as a forum in which ministers hear arguments about their own proposals and impose their own decisions. But there is also some opportunity for Parliament to act as a true legislature, when it deals with bills proposed by its own back-bench Members. Every MP may introduce a bill at any time. Several dozens of such Private Members' bills are proposed each year but make no progress because no time is provided for their debate. But about six Fridays a year are allocated for second reading debates on these bills proposed by back-bench MPs, and six more Fridays for the later stages of such bills which have passed second reading and committee. Priority on these Private Members' Fridays is allocated by a ballot.

Private Members' bills usually deal with matters about which Governments do not wish to legislate because they involve personal conscience or private behaviour. Votes are free, but without any instructions from the Whips MPs often go off to their constituencies on Private Members' Fridays, so the attendance is very small. Nevertheless, since 1965 several important reforms have been introduced in this way, including the abolition of the death penalty and the liberalisation of the laws concerning divorce, abortion and censorship of obscenity. In most years about ten Private Members' bills are enacted into law.

death penalty : peine de mort
abortion : divorce
Censorship of obscenity :

41

9 Control of Government Expenditure, Taxation and Administration

Parliament has other things to do as well as pass bills. The Government cannot legally spend any money without the permission of the House of Commons. This permission is given in the form of Acts of Parliament authorising the payment of sums of money out of the consolidated fund, which can be regarded as the Government's central bank account.

Before the annual Appropriation Bill is passed the House of Commons votes on some two hundred items of expenditure, but this is done in a few minutes. Only the Government is allowed to propose expenditure. The House still discusses the merits of the policies, but does not try to discuss the cost. But the Public Accounts Committee, chaired by a prominent Opposition MP, examines the departmental accounts in detail, with the help of the National Audit Office, and its reports are often critical of waste.

The House of Commons still keeps in close contact with taxation. Each year the taxes are authorised by a Finance Act, which is based on the Budget presented by the Chancellor of the Exchequer in March. In the detailed discussions Members try to persuade the Chancellor to reduce particular taxes, and they are not always unsuccessful.

The House of Commons spends more hours in session each year than any other parliamentary assembly, but for most of the time less than fifty MPs are present listening to the one who is speaking.

About one-seventh of this time is taken by senior and junior ministers stating the Government's policy or replying to questions and arguments put by the Opposition or by backbenchers of all parties. Rather less time is taken by Opposition front-bench spokesmen. The rest, about three-quarters, is occupied by backbenchers of all parties.

During any year almost every aspect of the nation's business is dealt with in debate. The average backbencher makes about five fifteen-minute speeches in a year, usually to a nearly empty chamber, but heard by ministers from the department responsible for the matter about which he is speaking. Some backbenchers' speeches are based on material supplied by national or local interests, and a large proportion deal with matters of concern to the MPs' own constituents. Back-bench speeches hardly ever influence the voting, though ministers may be impressed by what they hear, and sometimes modify their policies accordingly. Most back-benchers' arguments have already been put before departments through other contacts outside Parliament, or in private party committees; but the fact that they are put forward in open debate obliges the minister to listen and react.

For a long time it was argued that the House of Commons ought to have a system of committees, corresponding with the main government departments. After a series of experiments over many years, a system of this kind was at last created in 1979–80.

Each of these select committees has a more or less permanent membership, so that it can develop a thorough knowledge of the general problems associated with the work of its department. There are special advisers from outside Parliament, and individual members may employ their own research assistants. When a committee decides on a particular investigation, its clerk asks the department for a memorandum and statistics, and civil servants are called before the committee to answer questions. People from outside the administration may also be called in. The question sessions are held in public, and a stenographic record of the proceedings is published. Finally, the committee prepares and publishes a report, which may suggest changes in the way things have been done. Some reports are discussed in the press or debated in the House, and some have some real influence – partly because committee members usually forget about their parties in this work. But in their constituencies MPs get more reward for ideological vigour than for less glamorous work in committees.

10   The Competition for Power between the Parties

The evidence of opinion polls indicates that about half the British people are not regular supporters of any political party, but change their preference from time to time for various reasons. The rest are about equally divided, so about a quarter of the people are firm and committed Conservatives, another quarter firmly Labour and perhaps 5 per cent firm centrists.

The Labour Party was founded by the trade unions to represent the working class, and its most solid support comes from people who consider themselves to be working class, together with some intellectuals, often graduates working in the public sector, particularly in education and the social services. The hard core of the Conservatives' supporters is mainly middle class. Geographically the Labour Party's strength is concentrated in the most industrialised areas of the north, and above all in Scotland and South Wales. These areas, together with a few parts of London, cover almost a third of the constituencies in Britain, which Labour can be sure of winning. In these same areas there has been little support for the centre and Green parties. The Conservatives' 200 or more safe seats are a little more vulnerable to a strong centre party.

The result of a general election is decided by the swing of votes among the uncommitted people in the constituencies in which the support for the two major parties is more evenly divided. Of course, each of these uncommitted voters has a complex motivation, comprising judgments about the personalities of party leaders and about economic and social issues. Some take politics seriously and weigh the claims of the rival parties very thoroughly; others can easily be influenced by particular matters which have been brought into prominence by recent events. Frequent opinion polls, published in the media, give a fairly reliable indication of people's current preferences between the parties.

Through the polls, public opinion probably contributed to Mrs Thatcher's downfall. For most of 1989 and 1990 most polls put Labour in the lead, often by at least ten per cent. A new system of financing local government, by flat-rate taxes, inspired by Mrs Thatcher, produced riotous demonstrations in the streets. Attempts to make schools and the health service more businesslike were not well received. High interest rates caused distress to business and to people who had bought their homes with borrowed money, yet failed to prevent inflation from increasing steadily. Many Conservative MPs disliked Mrs Thatcher's dominant style and her negative attitude to the European Community. One by one, four ministers resigned from her government.

In November 1990 the deputy Prime Minister resigned, and Michael Heseltine, who had himself angrily resigned four years before, put himself forward as a rival candidate for the party leadership.

Under the party's rules its 372 MPs then had to decide by voting, if necessary in three ballots, whether or not Mrs Thatcher should be replaced by a new leader.

At the first ballot (with 16 abstentions) Mrs Thatcher led by 204 to 152. But her lead of 52 was two less than the 15 per cent of the 372 entitled to vote required by the rules for victory at this stage. The figures suggested that if she contested the second ballot the party would be unlikely to regain a spontaneous sense of unity.

Mrs Thatcher then withdrew, and gave her support to John Major, one of the two ministers who joined in the contest for the second ballot, which eventually gave 185 votes to Mr Major, 131 to Mr Heseltine and 56 to Mr Hurd, the Foreign Secretary. The vote for Major was so close to the overall majority needed for victory at this stage that the others withdrew. So Mr Major became party leader and Prime Minister, at the age of 47.

Before the first ballot a Mori opinion poll, reported in *The Times*, found that if Mrs Thatcher stayed as party leader Labour's percentage lead over the Conservatives would be 45–41, but if Heseltine replaced her the Conservatives would have a lead over Labour of 49–39. Other polls put the Conservatives ahead with either Heseltine or Major as party leader, but not with Mrs Thatcher. It looked as if a change of party leader might help the Conservatives to win the next general election – and help several dozen MPs to keep seats which they would be more likely to lose if Mrs Thatcher stayed. However, at the first stage many MPs were pressed by their constituency activists to support Mrs Thatcher. Before deciding how to vote they had to balance such opinions against their own and the findings of the polls about the preferences of the public.

Although Mr Major had been the candidate preferred by those Conservatives who were most supportive of Mrs Thatcher's right-wing policies, he quickly made conciliatory gestures, not only to those who had opposed him, but to the Labour Party. Mr Heseltine returned to the cabinet and at once proposed to try to find a generally-agreed solution to the problems of local government (for which he became responsible). It seemed that the 1990s might be less remarkable than the previous decade for the politics of confrontation.

Questions

TABLE 2.1

General Election Results 1945–1987

	Conservative		Labour		Liberal		Ruling party	Prime Minister
	Votes %	Seats	Votes %	Seats	Votes %	Seats		
July 1945	39.8	213	47.8	393	9	12	Lab.	Attlee
Feb. 1950	43.5	298	46.1	315	9	9	Lab.	Attlee
Oct. 1951	48.0	321	48.8	295	2.5	6	Con.	Churchill
May 1955	49.7	344	46.4	277	2.7	6	Con.	Eden (1957: Macmillan)
Oct. 1959	49.4	365	43.8	258	5.9	6	Con.	Macmillan (1963: Douglas-Home)
Oct. 1964	43.4	304	44.1	317	11.2	9	Lab.	Wilson
Mar. 1966	41.9	253	47.9	363	8.5	12	Lab.	Wilson
Oct. 1970	46.1	330	43.0	287	7.7	6	Con.	Heath
Feb. 1974	37.8	297	37.1	301	19.3	14	Lab.	Wilson
Oct. 1974	35.8	277	39.2	319	18.3	13	Lab.	Wilson (1976: Callaghan)
May 1979	43.9	339	37.0	269	13.8	11	Con.	Thatcher
Jun. 1983	42.4	397	27.6	209	25.4	23	Con.	Thatcher
May 1987	42.3	376	30.8	229	22.6	22	Con.	Thatcher

This table omits the votes gained by nationalist parties in Wales and Scotland (see Chapter 14), and by various minor parties, none of which have ever gained as much as 1 per cent of the votes.

Up to 1970 the Conservative and Labour figures include Northern Irish parties which were until then allied with one or the other. Since 1972 Northern Ireland's parties have been wholly separate and the figures for 1974 and after omit them.

1   In general, what matters of interest arise from a study of the figures, particularly since 1974?

2   Is this electoral system defensible?

TABLE 2.2

1987 General Election results in southern England

	Total seats	Conservatives			Labour			Alliance		
		Votes %	Seats won	% of seats	Votes %	Seats won	% of seats	Votes %	Seats won	% of seats
Inner London	31	37	13	42	42	17	55	19	1	3
Outer London	53	51	45	85	26	6	11	20	2	4
Rest of south-east	108	56	107	99	17	1	1	27	0	0
South-west	48	51	44	91	16	1	2	33	3	7
Whole of south	240	52	209	87	21	25	10	27	6	3

3   Would you agree that these figures specially illustrate the difficulties faced by a third party whose support is not concentrated, but widely spread?

4   In four-fifths of these southern constituencies won by the Conservatives the Alliance had between 20 and 42 per cent of the votes, and had more votes than Labour. The situation was similar at the election of 1983.

　　a)   Could it then be said that, while Britain as a whole had essentially a two-party system, Conservative–Labour, the south's system was Conservative–Alliance?

　　b)   Why did the Alliance collapse in 1987–88? Can you show the extent of its collapse? In what circumstances might it recover?

5   What advantages or disadvantages do you see in the survival of the monarchy?

6   Would you agree with those people who think that there should be a written constitution, as in other countries?

or

6a   Why does Britain, unlike other countries, have no written constitution? Ought one to be introduced?

7   Does the system put too much power in the hands of the Prime Minister?

or

7a   What are the factors which tend to build up the Prime Minister's personal power in the British political system? Is this power excessive?

8   Discuss the civil servants' duty of loyalty to their political chiefs.

The House of Lords.

3

The House of Lords

1   Ancient but Revived

When people talk of 'Parliament' they often mean 'the House of Commons'. The second chamber, the House of Lords, has almost no real powers at all, and it is generally agreed that with its present mainly hereditary composition it could not properly use any real power in a modern democratic state. It existed long before the House of Commons, and the basis of its membership has changed very little in 900 years. The Archbishops of Canterbury and York and twenty-four bishops of the Church of England are still members, as they were long ago. The survival of these ancient forms gives some good illustrations of the nature and development of the constitutional system. The Sovereign's throne is in the House of Lords' chamber, and the Queen sits on it once a year to make her speech, prepared by the Government, at the opening of an annual session of Parliament.

The House of Lords has no elected members and no fixed numbers. Apart from the bishops of the Church of England, who hold seats until they retire, all its members are lords who hold peerages. About one-third of these have been made peers by personal appointment for their own lives, and two-thirds are peers by heredity in one of five ranks: Duke, Marquess, Earl, Viscount and Baron. Nearly 800 have inherited their peerages from ancestors who were ennobled by the Crown, and nearly 400 others have themselves been given peerages by the Queen on the advice of a prime minister. All these peers keep their seats until they die, with no provision for expulsion or retirement. Those who hold hereditary peerages will be succeeded by their heirs, but since 1958 nearly all new peerages have been non-hereditary.

Two rationalisations were made by statute around 1960. Until 1958 there was a rule, based only on custom, that if a new peerage was given to a man, it must be inherited by his eldest son and then by *his* eldest son, and

49

so on indefinitely. For 100 years it had been agreed that this rule was inconvenient, because most new grants of peerages increased the future membership of the House. The Life Peerages Act of 1958 made it lawful to give peerages for the lifetime of their holders only, without inheritance, to women as well as men. It also gave seats in the House of Lords to about twenty women holding hereditary peerages in their own right, and to more than eighty hereditary peers of Scotland, who had previously elected sixteen of their number at each general election.

Since 1958 about twenty new peerages have been given each year (with big variations), nearly half of them to ex-ministers or other people who have been members of the House of Commons, the others to academics, doctors, trade union officials, businessmen and people with other types of experience. Most, but not all, have been aged over fifty and have been quite prominent in their various professions.

There are now about 400 'created' peers; about two-fifths of them are Labour Party supporters, the rest are equally divided between Conservatives and independents or centrists. About fifty are women, so this upper house, which until 1958 had no women members, now has more than the House of Commons. But there are still nearly 800 holders of hereditary peerages, half of which are less than 100 years old, and a quarter go back to various dates between 1283 and 1800.

A second modernisation was the introduction of payment of allowances paid to peers for each day's attendance at the House, together with other expenses including travel. A peer who attends every day gets much less than an MP.

Another change was a law of 1963 making it possible for a peer to renounce his peerage and so become eligible for election to the House of Commons. This law was a belated recognition of the reduced political status of this non-elected upper house. Until 1902, when Lord Salisbury resigned as Prime Minister, it was quite normal for the highest office to be held by a peer. By 1920 it was recognised that the Prime Minister needed to be in the elected House of Parliament, along with the great majority of other members of the Cabinet.

The power of the House of Lords was formally restricted by the Parliament Acts of 1911 and 1949. It has no powers at all with 'money bills'; bills enabling the Government to spend money or collect taxes go directly to the Queen for her formal approval after passing the Commons. Any other bill must pass both Houses, and if the Lords fail to agree to it in a form acceptable to the Commons by the end of a session of Parliament, the Commons may approve it again in the next session and send it to the Queen for her approval. As the new session begins a few days after the end of the previous one, the Lords can in practice delay the enactment of a bill by a few months.

The Lords have not used even this small power intentionally for over thirty years with any bill proposed by the Government. They have been restrained by other considerations more inhibiting than the formal rules. First, if they were seriously to obstruct policies of a Government supported by the Commons, the Prime Minister could give peerages to a few hundred supporters to ensure a majority in the Lords for the party. (A threat to do this in 1910–11 was enough to persuade the Conservative leadership to let the Parliament Bill pass into law.) Second, as there is no written constitution, a bill to abolish the House of Lords could be passed under the terms of the existing Parliament Act. Third, a Government with a majority in the Commons could reasonably claim that one of these drastic actions was justified because of the undemocratic composition of the House, and because, as most hereditary peers are Conservative supporters, the existence of a permanent potential one-party Conservative majority ensures that any attempt to exercise real power would have a dubious moral legitimacy.

Very few people seriously defend the hereditary system for a House of Parliament in a modern state. All parties, including the Conservatives, have produced plans for a new second chamber, with various mixtures of nominated and elected members. In 1968–69 the Lords themselves agreed to a reform bill put forward by the Labour government, but the bill was abandoned in the House of Commons. Because it dealt with a constitutional matter its details had to be discussed, without a time limit, on the floor of the House instead of in a standing committee. Some Labour left-wing MPs wanted to have the second chamber abolished altogether, and strongly opposed any reform which would increase its democratic legitimacy. A few right-wing Conservatives opposed any interference with the existing system. After these opponents had used up several days the Government gave priority to other business which it needed urgently to complete, and the debates on the bill to reform the Lords were still unfinished when the session ended. This experience discouraged any future attempts at reform, so nothing has been done.

In fact the still surviving unreformed House of Lords has become a vigorous and useful element in the political system, particularly in the 1980s, with a Conservative government in office. Most of the work is done by people who have been given peerages, rather than by those who have inherited them. Although more than 1,100 people have peerages, and are personally summoned to attend the House of Lords, nearly half of them attend on less than ten days a year, out of about 150 days of sitting. A third never attend at all. About 200 attend nearly every day, another 100 at least half the days of sitting and 300 between a tenth and half the days. The daily average varies between 200 and 400, slightly less than half of them Conservatives, a quarter Labour and a third centrists or non-party people. At most times there are more women present than in the House of Commons. As a body representing the people as a whole the working House of Lords is in some ways better than the House of Commons in which mutually hostile men of the Conservative and Labour Parties are more predominant than in the nation as a whole.

In the House of Lords party hostility is reasonably restrained, and common rules of politeness are well observed. The normal Monday to Thursday sittings begin with questions to the Government, after which the business proceeds as arranged informally between the whips of the parties and non-party peers. For many debates an order of speaking is published in advance. There are few formal rules. The Lord Chancellor or his deputy sits on the Woolsack (a sort of pouffe below the Sovereign's throne), but does nothing to impose order, and does not even call on people to speak.

The arrangement of the seats in the Lords chamber is similar to that in the Commons. Long, straight blocks of benches face each other with Government supporters on one side and Opposition parties on the other. The bishops' bench is on the Government side. But at one end of the chamber, unlike the Commons, there are 'cross-benches' for non-party peers.

The Government front bench is occupied by peers who hold office, with the peer concerned with the current business at the Dispatch Box. Most big departments are represented by junior ministers, as their chiefs are in the Commons and cannot be in the Lords chamber except as silent spectators. Five peers hold office as Lords in Waiting and take part as government spokesmen instructed by civil servants. The Government Chief Whip is Captain of the Honourable Corps of Gentlemen-at-Arms, assisted by the Captain of the Queen's Bodyguard of the Yeomen of the Guard, though both these offices are sometimes held by women. As with so many other things, ancient offices, now archaic, have been adapted to a modern function.

It is often said that the House of Lords is at its best in its debates, without vote, on topics of general interest, at least once a week. Whatever the topic, there are speeches by great experts, including some who do not often take part in the business of the House but come in only for debates which interest them. These speeches have no obvious or definable result, but ministers and civil servants may hear them, or read them in the stenographic record (Lords *Hansard*) and may be influenced. Part of these proceedings also go out on television, sometimes live but more often in edited and recorded programmes, and the serious newspapers report them. These debates are part of the general process of discussion in the nation as a whole, and may stimulate government action. But the House spends most of its time on the detailed consideration of the Government's bills. Important bills go to the Lords after passing the Commons; some uncontroversial bills go through the Lords before the Commons, so as to balance the timetables of the two Houses during a session of Parliament.

With each bill brought from the Commons the Lords debate the principles on second reading but normally agree without any formal vote. Their main work is to approve or reject proposals to amend bills, after discussions which include statements of the Government's wishes, made by a minister from the front bench.

Whatever the party in power, the House makes most decisions without voting, according to the Government's advice, but votes ('divisions') have become much more frequent since the 1960s. When Labour has been in power nearly all divisions have resulted in defeat for the Government. But most of the controversial amendments made to Labour government bills have then been cancelled by the House of Commons, and the Conservative leaders in the Lords have advised their supporters to accept the Commons' decisions. In 1974–79 the Labour Party, in power, resented the trouble and delay caused by this process, and in a few cases ministers were obliged to abandon or modify parts of their policies. But a policy to abolish the House of Lords, approved by a Labour Party Conference, has not been included in the party's election manifestos.

In the 1980s Mrs Thatcher's government could never be sure of winning divisions in the House of Lords. In ten years the Government was defeated more than 100 times, when Opposition peers were joined by large numbers of independents – and sometimes a few Conservatives too – in voting for amendments to its bills against its wishes. In some cases ministers advised the Commons majority to accept changes made by the Lords against their own policies. But before some debates on particularly controversial matters, the whips were successful in persuading large numbers of Conservative 'backwoodsmen' to come in and vote with their ministers. 'Backwoodsmen' are typically peers who have inherited their peerages, support the Conservative Party, but do not normally bother to go to the House of Lords. Some recent Conservative government victories, helped by backwoodsmen's votes, have revived the old argument that the upper house is just a tool of the Conservative Party.

One of the oldest functions of the House of Lords is judicial, though now this is ancillary to its essential role. Its work as the highest and final Court of Appeal is now done in a fairly small room of the Palace of Westminster, where the court consists of five of the senior judges to whom peerages have been given. The ten Lords of Appeal in Ordinary are also full members for life of the House of Lords as a legislative body, so both the active and retired judicial lords may sit, speak and vote. Some of them do so, usually on matters concerning the administration of the law.

2   Titles and Honours

British titles are complicated and confusing. Most of the hereditary peers who are dukes, earls or marquesses and some other peers have titles differing from their family names. Most people to whom peerages are given use their family names for their titles, but if there is already a peer of the same name they must add 'of (some place)'. So the former Prime Minister Wilson became Lord Wilson of Rievaulx. But his predecessor Macmillan became Earl of Stockton (a town which he once represented in the Commons). He was the first person since 1964 to receive a hereditary peerage to which there was an heir.

Some people with the title 'Lord' are not peers and not members of the House of Lords. In Scotland all judges of the higher courts are Lords (but not peers) and in England and Wales the judges of the Court of Appeal (below the House of Lords) have the judicial title Lord Justice. The sons and daughters of some hereditary peers of the higher ranks have the 'courtesy' title Lord or Lady, which is used with the first name except with the eldest sons of some families. Other sons and daughters of peers are called 'the Honourable', a title not to be confused with 'the Right Honourable', which is used for the (roughly) 400 members of the Privy Council.

State honours, including peerages, are awarded twice a year, on 1st January and on the Queen's official birthday in June. More than 100 men are made Knights (for life) each year, and there are about 3,000 Knights now living. They are called Sir – (first name) – surname. Sir Geoffrey Howe, who was Foreign Secretary from 1983 to 1989, may be called 'Sir Geoffrey' or plain 'Howe', but not 'Sir Howe'. The female equivalent is 'Dame', but Knights outnumber Dames by more than ten to one. These titles bring no special privileges and are not hereditary, though until the 1960s a few hereditary baronetcies were given each year, and there are a few hundred 'Sirs' who have inherited their titles.

Every honours list includes many civil servants and military officers, with knighthoods and lower honours carefully graded in several Orders, such as the Order of the Bath. The biggest of these is the Order of the British Empire, and the graded distinctions of CBE, OBE and MBE are distributed to hundreds of citizens who are considered to have done good work in their jobs or in voluntary organisations or local government. The Prime Minister is responsible for advising the Queen on the award of all these honours. Some are given for political reasons, but most are non-political, awarded through a network of civil servants who sift suggestions put to them from innumerable sources.

A few people, mainly politicians of the Left, despise the honours system. Labour prime ministers have given more peerages but fewer other honours to their own political supporters. Otherwise the system has worked with little change, whatever the party currently in power. Companies and other organisations like to have names with titles or letters after them among their officials or directors.

A cabinet minister who would like to have a peerage on leaving office can usually have one, even if the resignation is involuntary – but only at a time when the by-election needed to fill the vacated House of Commons seat is not inconvenient to the ruling party. Conservative prime ministers give knighthoods (more rarely peerages) to back-bench MPs who have served the party long and well. The prospect of an honour stimulates chiefs of boards, like health authorities, to be assiduous in doing their work and in implementing government policy. Some honours are wholly non-political. A few (including peerages) are given on the proposal of the Leader of the Opposition, who then expects hard work for the party in the House of Lords in return. Most importantly, the power of choosing people to be honoured is extremely useful to the Prime Minister and Government, and to the whole hierarchy of administration. A knighthood, CBE, etc. brings both prestige and some improved prospects of influence and good jobs.

People who receive awards enjoy the process of receiving them. They go to Buckingham Palace to receive them from the Queen at a ceremony called an investiture. Their relatives who go with them like it too. The state's honours share some of the magic of royalty, which still holds most British people in its spell.

3   Membership of the House of Lords

There is no simple answer to the question 'how many members of the House of Lords are there?' Nearly 1,200 people, including more than sixty women, are entitled to membership. Nearly two-thirds have inherited their peerages from their fathers or earlier ancestors in direct line of descent, and are described as 'peers by succession'. But when a person inherits a peerage on the death of a father, uncle or cousin, he (or she) must first prove a right to the succession. In most, but not all, cases this is quite simple. Once this has been done, the new peer receives a 'writ of summons' from the Queen, commanding attendance at Parliament, and may then go to the House to be formally admitted as a member, with some ceremony.

It is estimated that nearly a hundred people who would be entitled to 'join' the House of Lords have not gone through these processes, and so are not members. More than a hundred others have gone through the processes but then applied for leave of absence – though if they change their minds they may have the leave of absence cancelled. Others who are full members never attend, some of them because they are too old or ill.

During the course of a year between 700 and 800 individuals actually attend at the House at least once. An analysis of those who attended in a recent session is useful for an understanding of the nature of this curious institution. The figures given below, for the session 1984–85, are extracted or adapted from Donald Shell's book *The House of Lords* (1988).

There are two main categories of members of the House:

1) those who *succeeded* to hereditary peerages, and thus hold their seats by right of succession
2) those who have been *created* as peers (or bishops); that is, those on whom peerages, with the right to sit in the House of Lords, have been conferred by the Crown on the advice of the Prime Minister in office at the time of the conferment.

These include four subcategories, as below, with numbers in May 1987:

a) Life peers created since 1958   346

b) Life peers created as Law Lords   21

   (10 currently active as appeal judges, 11 retired)

c) People created as hereditary peers, to be   26
succeeded by their eldest children if any. Only one new hereditary peerage was conferred in 1964–90 on a person with an heir (former Prime Minister Macmillan), so this group is now declining fast.

d) The Archbishops of Canterbury and York,   26
     the bishops of Durham, London and
     Winchester, and the 21 other most senior
     bishops of the Church of England – all being
     members of the House of Lords only until
     retirement.

Questions

TABLE 3.1

Numbers who attended at least two-thirds of the sittings (100–151) in 1984–85

	Created	Inherited	TOTAL
Conservative	38	64	102
Labour	54	5	59
'Centre'	23	11	34
Non-party	16	22	38

1   'With no written constitution, and with an electoral system that regularly gives power to a party supported by a minority of the people, Britain needs a strong second house of Parliament.'
What do you think about this? Should there be an elected second chamber with more real power than the House of Lords?

2   Why has the Labour left wing regularly wanted to abolish the House of Lords?

3   What are your opinions about the inclusion in a house of parliament of many people who attend only rarely?

A public library in London.

4

Local Government

1 The Permanent Principles

Although the United Kingdom is a unitary state, not a federal one, a very large part of the public services are administered by elected local councils, (local authorities), which together employ more than two million people. The central government employs only one-third of this number. Scotland and Northern Ireland have their own systems, which are not quite the same as that of England and Wales, though the differences are only superficial. For the sake of simplicity, this chapter will deal only with England and Wales.

All local authorities derive their existence and their powers and functions from Parliament and the central government. Parliament can take powers away or add to them, and it can even abolish any particular authority, or group or class of authorities, if it wants to. The Local Government Act of 1972 reorganised the whole system, bringing a new structure into effect in 1974. This was partly revised in 1986.

Although Parliament has these powers over local authorities, and has used them recently, it does not exercise any detailed supervision through any office of the nature of prefect or local governor. Many of the activities of local authorities are in fact supervised, advised or controlled by the central government, but there is no single agency of control for any particular local authority or class of authorities. In each area the elected council and its officers have direct relations with the various central government departments – though these may have regional offices through which some of the central–local relations are conducted.

Traditionally, the most important local area is the county. England has been divided into counties for more than 1,000 years. Most of them, except those near the outer edges of England, have the old word 'shire' in their names e.g. Yorkshire. In each county the Queen appoints a Lord Lieutenant as her representative, now only for ceremonial purposes.

Except around London these ancient (or 'historic') counties kept their boundaries unchanged until 1974, when some of them lost territory to newly created counties, some of which in their turn became obsolete in 1986.

Within the counties the oldest units are the parishes. These are the local communities or villages which became established in the Middle Ages, each with a church as its focal point. They have their equivalents all over Europe, such as French *communes* and German *Gemeinden*. Until 1888 they were important units of administration. Although they still survive and have elected parish councils they now have almost no powers of their own.

From the early Middle Ages, as some villages grew into towns, the Crown gave them 'charters of incorporation' as 'boroughs' or 'cities', with their own mayors and councils. But from the late nineteenth century successive changes have been imposed by Parliament. Some old boroughs have been expanded, some, absorbed by others, have ceased to exist as distinct units of administration, and some have survived with little change.

2   The Structure since 1986

There are now two types of structure. One, created in 1974 and changed in 1986, applies to Greater London and the six other largest urban areas, which are sometimes called conurbations. The other applies to all the rest of England, with most of its area and three-fifths of its population, and to the whole of Wales.

London

Greater London, with nearly seven million people, consists of thirty-two 'London boroughs' and the City of London. Most of these boroughs have between 150,000 and 300,000 people. The best known of these is the City of Westminster. At the centre the City of London survives as an independent unit, with less than 10,000 resident inhabitants, half a million office workers by day and a few thousand visitors to the Tower, Guildhall and St Paul's Cathedral at weekends. The Lord Mayor of London is concerned only with this small area. In all other parts the boroughs' elected councils run all the services except a few which necessarily concern them all. The buses and underground railways are now run by the London Transport Executive, responsible to the central government, and the Home Secretary is in charge of the Metropolitan Police (the police force in London).

A Greater London County was created in 1965, absorbing the whole county of Middlesex and the suburban parts of four other counties, but the council and functions of this county were abolished in 1986. A 'London Residuary Body' was set up to manage the business of handing over the County's functions and property to the boroughs or other agencies.

Conurbations

The six main city areas in the midlands and north of England have local systems similar to London's. These areas, around Birmingham, Manchester, Liverpool, Sheffield, Leeds and Newcastle upon Tyne, have between one and three million people each. They became metropolitan counties in 1974, but these new counties lost their councils and all their functions in 1986. Now each county's area consists of boroughs, one of which is the central city, the others being based on the surrounding satellite towns, each expanded so as to include the areas between (which are now mainly built-up). The borough councils run all the local services except police, public transport and a few others which have joint agencies.

Shire counties

England outside London and these 'conurbations' consists of thirty-nine 'shire' counties. Most of these are the old historic or geographic counties, though the smallest pairs have been joined together. Some others lost territory and population to the metropolitan counties in 1974. Also around three river mouths new 'shire' counties were created, each including parts of two old counties.

The thirty-nine 'shire' counties are responsible for the main local functions, such as education, social services and police. Each is divided into 'districts' (typically about seven per county) which provide housing, refuse collection and other services best managed on a smaller scale. In general, most towns with more than about 80,000 people within these counties have become districts, but outside these towns the district divisions are new creations, normally including a few towns and several dozen rural parishes, all of which have elected councils but very few functions. Some districts are called by the names of their biggest towns, others have newly-invented names chosen by their councils, often after prolonged argument.

In 1974 Wales was reorganised more thoroughly than England. Twelve of the counties with small populations were merged into five, all with new Welsh names; the thirteenth, Glamorgan in the industrial south, with half the Welsh population, was divided into three. Some old counties became districts of the new merged counties; other districts were new creations, among them Ogwr, Dwyfor and Glyndwr.

3   The Working of Local Government

Local councillors are elected for four-year terms, and in May of every year some local elections take place. For the counties and some districts the complete councils are elected at four-year intervals, but for other districts (including most of those which are big towns) and for metropolitan boroughs the elections are phased so that only one-third of the councillors are elected together in each year, except the years when county elections are held.

Each councillor represents a 'ward'. Within each council's area the wards are supposed to be as far as practicable equal in population, so their boundaries have to be revised from time to time – though in districts there may be some double or bigger wards with two or more seats each. There is no proportionality in the voting; as with the House of Commons the candidate with most votes wins the seat. In rural districts several small parishes may together form a ward; a big town is divided into many wards. The wards have no function except as divisions for electoral purposes, but political party organisations based on wards may have influence on their own ward councillors.

In most local elections only about half of the people use their right to vote, and voting is dominated by the national parties. For some councils, including those of most inner London boroughs and big northern towns, every election leaves Labour with an absolute majority of the seats, others are permanently Conservative, but in many others in the 1980s the biggest party held less than half of the seats, with centrists holding the balance. The situation with a single-party majority tends to be very different from that when a middle party is in a position to prevent domination by majority – and the way councils work tends to reinforce this obvious difference.

Every local council has its presiding officer, chosen by the whole council for one year only. In metropolitan and London boroughs the presiding officer has the title Mayor or Lord Mayor; so too in those districts which are called 'boroughs' or 'cities'. In other districts, and in counties, the presiding officer is called 'chairman'. The title Lord Mayor is used in the seventeen most important English cities and in Cardiff in Wales, but a Lord Mayor does not receive any title personally by virtue of the office.

The Lord Mayor of London in his ceremonial coach.

A mayor or lord mayor is surrounded by some colourful ceremonial as the town's first citizen. In a big city there may be an official residence, a grand car, and (for use a few times a year) an even grander but less comfortable carriage pulled by four horses and accompanied by outriders and buglers. Ordinary mayors have ceremonial duties too, and in these functions the role of the mayoress still survives – either the mayor's wife or a daughter, sister, niece or friend of a mayor who is a woman or unmarried man.

It is only for ceremonial and social purposes that a mayor is first citizen. The office, being held only for a year, does not give its holder any significant position of political leadership. The mayor's main task, apart from ceremony, is to preside over full meetings of the council, which are not frequent, during his one-year term of office. Real political leadership belongs to the person who is chosen to be the leader of the majority party, if there is one.

In districts which are not 'boroughs' or 'cities' (and in counties) the chairman of the council usually has a similar status but less ceremonial. Mayors and chairmen are chosen each year by vote of the whole council, but often there is no need for a vote because the choice has been agreed in advance through private discussion between the parties. In some cases these offices are held by councillors of the different parties in turn.

All local councils work through committees. Each council has a committee for each of the main sections of its work; for example the general management of the schools in a county or a metropolitan district is under the control of the education committee of the county or district council. Some of the committees consist only of members of the council (with the parties represented in the same proportion as in the whole council), and some of them have in addition a few co-opted members, i.e. people who do not belong to the council but have been chosen to assist the committee with their special knowledge or other qualifications. For very important matters the committee can only recommend to the council what is to be done, and the decision is made by the council in general session. Meetings are normally open to the public.

The local authorities appoint their own staffs. At the middle and higher levels of the local government service the local government officers are usually ready to move from one place to another, and it is often necessary to move in order to get promotion. The appointment of the local councils' staffs is supposed to have nothing to do with politics, though inevitably politics may have something to do with some of the top appointments. If the political majority of a council changes as a result of an election, it is not to be expected that there will be changes among the professional staff as a result.

The chairman of a committee (for example, on social services or education) has to work closely with the departmental chiefs and senior officers. Individual problems and matters of detail tend to be settled by the officers, though members of the public who are aggrieved can try to get their ward councillors to intervene. Officers' decisions, like those of civil servants, have to agree with the main policies laid down by their committees. The real influence of the officers, as distinct from the elected councillors, varies greatly from one council or department to another. A committee chairman may be dominant or not. The experience and skill of the politician is an important factor; so too the amount of time spent on council work. If a single party dominates the council it may give the chairs of all the committees to its own party members, and this strengthens the position of the chairmen. A committee chairman also works closely with elected councillors who belong to the same party. Both for committee business and for general council business there may be private party meetings at which the party's position is decided, and strict discipline is imposed on party members. Party discipline is often very strong in councils with Labour majorities, and in some cases the Labour councillors' meetings are the main power centres.

Most local expenditure goes on services which councils are required by law to provide, though they provide other services too. Part of the money needed is given to them in the form of grants from the central government, fixed by complex formulae and paid for out of national tax revenues. In the economic crisis of 1975 the Labour government began to restrict its local grants, and in the 1980s the Conservative government was even more restrictive, so that the proportion financed by central grants fell to much less than half of the total. After 1983 the Government took a new and unprecedented power to set limits also to the amounts that local councils could collect by their own local taxes, and soon afterwards began preparations to impose on them a completely new system of local taxation, designed to make the councils more accountable to their voters.

For the cost of running their services the local councils rely partly on grants from the central government, and partly on taxes which they collect from local residents and businesses which operate in their areas. The grants paid by the central government, from the proceeds of income tax and other centrally-collected taxes, are calculated to take account of local needs.

Until 1990 the local councils collected their own taxes based on the value of houses and other buildings. In 1990 a new law came into effect, replacing the property tax by a new tax called a 'community charge'. This is a fixed amount to be paid by each person to the local authorities, though some people are at least partly exempt. A person with a small income may pay only a proportion (a fifth or more) of the normal rate.

Each council estimates its costs for the next year, then decides how much it needs to collect from its residents after taking account of grants from the central government and other revenues. So the amount to be paid by each person depends on the expenditures of the borough or county and district where he or she lives. But the amount no longer depends on the value of the house.

The most obvious effect of the new tax is that people living in houses of high value are likely to pay less than before, while people in less valuable houses pay more. The Government hoped that as a result people would vote for local councillors promising to restrict expenditure. By 1990 it seemed that the real result was to increase the unpopularity of the Conservative government responsible for the new scheme.

This new tax is popularly called a 'poll tax'. That name revives the ancient poll tax of the 1370s, with its original meaning. 'Poll' is an ancient Middle English word meaning 'head' or 'person'. In that sense the word is now extinct; the more modern use, connected with counting votes or opinions, has caused some people to suppose, wrongly, that the new tax is a tax on voting in elections. The first poll tax of the 1370s was a major factor in producing the Peasants' Revolt of 1381, and a few later attempts at repeating the experiment were disastrous.

One problem for the 1990s is that there are several million people who do not just live in one place for the whole of a year. The number of possible variations is incalculable. The local councils need to spend vast amounts of money in paying officials to make decisions about the situation of the people whose liability to the tax needs to be defined.

Before changing the basis of local taxes, the central government had already increased its interference with the autonomy of local councils. In particular it restricted the amounts that local councils could collect from their people. Many local councils, including some with Conservative majorities, complained that it was impossible for them to provide local services of an acceptable quality without more funds. In 1990 Mr Major's government began a new review of the whole system. It decided that the new 'poll tax' would be replaced by a local tax based on the value of property. It also increased the proportion of local expenditure paid for out of central government taxation.

about unfair dismissal or disputed rights to social security benefits or to compensation for industrial injury or illness. Lawyers may be involved in these, and in some cases there may be appeals to the ordinary courts of law. But of all the adjudications needed in the modern world none arouse such wide interest as the public inquiries which hear objections to proposals for great new building projects, such as nuclear power stations, new roads, new housing schemes, hypermarkets or reservoirs. A big inquiry may take several months, with proposers and objectors represented by senior barristers. The total cost to all the parties may be several million pounds. When all the arguments have been presented the presiding officer, who may be a judge or barrister or civil servant, produces a decision based on a long and detailed summary balancing the favourable and unfavourable arguments.

2   Criminal Courts

There are two main kinds of courts, and two kinds of judicial officers to correspond with them. Courts of first instance are presided over by magistrates, who are normally Justices of the Peace (JPs); higher courts ('crown' courts) by judges, or in some cases, senior barristers specially appointed to perform judicial functions for part of their time.

Magistrates' Courts

Every person charged with an offence is summoned to appear before a local magistrates' court, which may impose a fine up to a general limit of £2,000 or twelve months' imprisonment, though for some specified offences the laws prescribe maximum penalties below these limits. With 98 per cent of cases the magistrates on the bench decide on guilt or innocence, and if necessary what penalty to impose. With more serious cases the magistrates can decide only to send them for trial in a crown court. A person accused before a magistrates' court may demand to be sent for trial before a crown court in some of the more serious cases with which in general the magistrates could have dealt themselves.

A magistrates' court normally consists of three Justices of the Peace (occasionally, two or four or more). The JPs are ordinary but worthy citizens who have been appointed to their positions by the Lord Chancellor on the advice of local appointing committees. JPs have no formal qualifications; they are chosen merely for their good reputation, often with the support of political parties or approved voluntary bodies. Once appointed, they are expected to attend courses of instruction about their work. There are 27,000 JPs in England; each of them works in the courts on about 30–50 days a year. Those who have jobs must take time off, and receive a small compensation for loss of earnings; but otherwise the JPs receive no payment for their work. Attempts are now being made to ensure that JPs are of widely differing social backgrounds, but inevitably most are middle class.

In their courts the JPs are advised on points of law by their Clerks, who are professional lawyers; otherwise they decide each case brought before them according to their sense of what is fair and suitable, within the limits of their powers, and with some attention to general guidance which they receive. There are a few special exceptions to the general pattern. Some of the courts in London and in some other big towns have stipendiary magistrates, who are qualified lawyers, work full time and are paid salaries; but there are only seventy stipendiary magistrates in England, and a few in Wales.

Crown Courts

About 2 per cent of criminal cases are sent up to crown courts. The most serious of these are dealt with before high court judges, the vast majority before circuit judges or senior barristers who spend only part of their time working as judges, the rest of it pleading as counsel on behalf of litigants.

In crown courts many people accused of offences plead 'guilty', so that the judge proceeds at once to hear excuses, or pleas in extenuation. At this stage too the court is told about any previous convictions. Either at once, or after taking time for thought, the judge pronounces sentence – prison, fine, probation or other treatment. People found guilty may have to contribute towards the cost of their trial, and to pay compensation to their victims.

If the plea is 'not guilty' there must be a trial. A large number of citizens is ordered to attend the court for jury service after being chosen by lot from the list of electors living in the area. Twelve people are chosen by lot from the waiting group to serve as a jury for the trial, but both the prosecution and the defence can reject up to seven of them. For some kinds of case defending counsel reject people who look too severe or even too soberly dressed. Also, any juror who knows anything about the accused person or the case must be replaced by another. Both judge and jury must try the case only on the evidence immediately relevant to it.

When the trial begins, the prosecution describes the crime with the help of questions answered by witnesses, who may then be questioned by defence counsel. Some of the prosecution witnesses may be police officers reporting what they saw, with evidence of fingerprints or searches. Statements made by the accused person after being arrested may be quoted only if the accused has been given the routine warning that the statement may be used as evidence.

The defence counsel then calls witnesses for the defence, including the accused if that seems useful. Either side may ask the judge to rule any evidence out of order, for example because it is indirect, or 'hearsay', that is, based on something told to the witness by another person.

When the presentation is finished, counsel on both sides make closing speeches, and finally the judge sums up for the benefit of the jury, tells them about points of law, and sends them out to decide their verdict, which cannot be 'guilty' except on the vote of at least ten of the twelve.

If the jury's verdict is 'guilty' the jury is dissolved and the process goes on as if the plea had been guilty. One fundamental assumption is that the accused person is innocent until guilt is proved or admitted. Anyone who is arrested may refuse to answer questions put by the police, or insist on answering only in the presence of a solicitor as a legal adviser – though it is now proposed that the police, in giving their evidence to a court, should be allowed to report a refusal to give answers.

No trial process can be perfect. Some people have been found guilty of crimes which they did not commit; and probably some who were really guilty have been found 'not guilty' and set free. There are two possible stages of appeal, and occasionally an appeal court rejects the conclusion of a trial, or alters the sentence imposed.

Justice, both civil and criminal, operates with reasonable speed. The magistrates' courts are often criticised on the ground that the Justices of the Peace are not professionally trained, but their critics may forget that the most important part of their work, that of imposing penalties on minor wrongdoers, is essentially social rather than legal in character. At the same time there is very much less complaint about the lack of social or criminological training of some of the high court judges, who have to pass sentence in the more serious cases. The main weakness of the legal system is the cost, though a system of legal aid pays poorer people's costs.

3 Crime and Punishment

Like many other countries, Britain has experienced a great increase in criminal activity of nearly every kind. Nearly five times as many acts of violence were reported to the police in 1987 as twenty years before. Although most burglars are not caught, those who are caught overload the courts and prisons. Although the courts try, in theory at least, to use probation, community service and other devices to avoid sentencing people to prison, the 50,000 people in prison are more, in proportion to the population, than in any other Western European country. Vast sums are being spent on building new prisons, but the prisons are still overcrowded, and the humiliation suffered by their inmates make rehabilitation difficult. Many prisoners are released early on parole.

The prisons in England are run by the Home Office, though each prison has a local Board of Visitors (some of them JPs) who make reports about conditions and also deal with serious bad behaviour. Normally prisoners are released after serving two-thirds, or less, of the time for which they were sentenced, but an offence in prison may be punished by the loss of some days of remission. There are several kinds of prisons, including open ones, and some prisoners go out to work in groups outside. Prisoners who want to study for examinations are helped to do so, and there are training courses in prison. But in practice some spend very little time outside their cells.

4　The Police

One of the most British institutions is the British policeman, with the odd helmet reminiscent of the topees that Europeans used to wear in India. To an Englishman a motorised policeman with a flat-topped hat looks somehow a little less reassuring than one with a helmet. Outside London the police are all local forces, employed and paid by police authorities based on counties. The central government gives the local authorities grants towards the cost of policing. Inspectors from the Home Office visit the local forces, and the Home Secretary can approve or disapprove of appointments and removals of Chief Constables, but the actions of a local police force are normally not the responsibility of any minister. In London the regime is different. The Metropolitan Police, whose zone of operation covers Greater London, is under the direct responsibility of the Home Secretary, as good order in the capital concerns the central government. The Metropolitan Police provides certain national police services, including the maintenance of a national record of all criminals and crimes, to which local police forces may refer. The famous 'Scotland Yard' is the Criminal Investigation Department, which gets its popular name from New Scotland Yard, where its offices are situated, close to Whitehall and the Houses of Parliament.

The policemen and women of today need a great variety of new professional skills to deal with modern crime and with the other problems which afflict life in Britain no less than other countries. Moving mostly in cars rather than on foot, the police are less obviously in contact with the public than in the past. When going about their normal work the police do

A policeman joining in the fun at London's Notting Hill carnival.

not carry guns: they themselves prefer to be unarmed.

The police come into the news from time to time when they have to deal with large-scale riots and other breaches of public order. During the coalminers' strike of 1984 huge crowds gathered outside some mines intending to prevent people from going to work. Hundreds of policemen were needed to control these crowds and to protect those who were regarded as strike breakers. In cases such as these a local police force may 'borrow' from other police forces. But only a few strikes have produced mass violence, which occurs much more often at football matches, or even among crowds of youths who have drunk too much on some Saturday night or public holiday.

Most people have a positive attitude to the police, and opinion polls have indicated that there is much public sympathy with men and women who have to deal with mob violence. There is a formal system through which complaints of police behaviour may be investigated, but in the late 1980s it was found that these procedures had not prevented some serious failures in the system of administering justice. Some Irish people had been convicted of a terrorist offence on the basis of confessions which had been improperly extracted from them, and the truth was discovered only after they had spent several years in prison.

There were other cases too in which there were grounds for suspecting that the police had persuaded people to confess to crimes which they had not committed. Some other inquiries revealed more cases of misconduct by the police.

Meanwhile, in the 1980s the central government increased its expenditures on the London police as well as its grants towards the cost of local police forces. The size of police forces was increased, and the pay of the police was increased more generously than that of many other workers in the public sector. But all this expenditure to promote 'law and order' has not stopped the growth of crime.

Questions

TABLE 5.1

Notifiable offences recorded by the police in England and Wales
(thousands)

Notifiable offences recorded	1971	1981	1986	1990
Violence against the person	47	100	125	182
Sexual offences	24	19	23	29
Burglary	451	723	932	945
Robbery	7	20	30	35
Theft and handling stolen goods	1,004	1,603	2,004	2,261
Fraud and forgery	100	107	133	141
Criminal damage	27	—	584	708
Other offences	6	4	17	30
TOTAL	1,666	2,577	3,847	4,326

1 As factors influencing the increase in crime, how would you assess the following?
  a) decline in respect for authority in general
  b) violence on television, films, etc.
  c) encouragement, through advertising, of excessive expectations
  d) unemployment
  e) other factors

2 Explain the difference, in England and Wales, between a magistrate (JP) and a judge.

3 What is your opinion about the use of people without legal training for judicial functions in magistrates' courts?

4 Does Britain seem to you to be backward in its treatment of offenders?

Buying and selling company shares in a stockbroker's office.

Members of the National Union of Teachers voting at their annual conference.

6

Work and Money

1 The Structure of the Economy

In every country the first resource is land, and densely-populated Britain has not much of it. About 2 per cent of the population work on farms, many of them tenants of big estates. After 1945 governments encouraged them, by advice and financial inducements, to use their land effectively, and when Britain joined the European Community in 1972 most farms were well equipped and mechanised.

Now their efficiency is embarrassing. Environmentalists complain that insecticides and fertilisers have polluted air and water. Vast lengths of hedges have been cut down, to the detriment of wild flowers and butterflies. Intensive methods of producing eggs and some kinds of meat are criticised; few pigs are to be seen wandering free. And too much food is being produced.

Although each year much good farmland is sold for building, farmers are encouraged to put some land to other uses, such as facilities for recreation. Hills once grazed by sheep are being used for forestry, encouraged by government grants – though there has been bitter complaint about the damage to the scenery and to the whole ecology caused by new coniferous forests.

But agriculture is a small part of the whole economy. For 200 years manufacturing has been more important, but by the 1970s it was clear that Britain's old manufacturing industries were less progressive than the same industries in other Western European countries. Newer industries, such as car manufacture, were no better than the older ones like textiles. Half the new cars on British roads were imported, mainly from France, West Germany and Italy, where few British cars were bought. In general the value of goods produced by a hundred workers had for many years increased much less than in West Germany. In some factories there was not enough new equipment; in others, new equipment was not being used efficiently. Some managers complained that when they brought in new equipment they had to spend more time negotiating with trade unions about changes in working processes than in running their businesses. Even so, strikes were frequent.

After 1979, when Mrs Thatcher's government came to power, there was less action by the state to help inefficient industries to survive, or to prevent the growth of unemployment. Within a few years hundreds of factories were demolished or taken over for new purposes. Some sections of the old industries improved their productivity and became more profitable than before, but some were less successful.

In 1979 many of the old industries were owned by the state. Their managing boards were told to aim at profit, and to prepare for being sold off to the private sector. Many steel plants were closed, and in a few years those which survived were no longer needing subsidies. Coal production was concentrated in the most efficient pits, including a few new ones. In 1989 most electric power was still generated in coal-fired power stations, but the government was sympathetic to plans to increase nuclear power.

No industry has suffered so great a change as shipbuilding, in which Britain led the world for 200 years or more. As recently as the 1920s British shipyards built half of the world's tonnage of new passenger and cargo ships. Nationalisation in 1976 failed to stop the industry's decline. Three years later its share of the world's output of new merchant ships was down to 5 per cent. In the 1980s it declined still further, to below 2 per cent, though the few surviving shipyards still had some work for various navies and the undersea oil industry. But the experience of shipbuilding was not typical; many other industries became more competitive in the 1980s.

New 'high-tech' industries developed, and there was a new diversity, with some growth of small-scale enterprise. While the number of people employed in manufacturing fell by a quarter in 1979–84, then by a little more in the next five years, manufacturing output rose substantially and many companies' profits doubled in the five years to 1989.

Two parallel developments have affected Britain slightly more than most other European countries. One is the increase in the service industries, as distinct from the productive ones. The other is the increase in the proportion of people in white collar as distinct from manual jobs. More than half of all working people, whether employees or self-employed, are now providing services. Although some service work is manual, less than half of all working people are in jobs traditionally associated with the working class.

There has been some growth in the number of people who work for schools and hospitals, social services, the police and prisons, and in public administration. But the biggest growth has been in finance, banking and insurance, along with 'other services', including the law, advertising, catering and entertainment. These growing categories now employ together four million people, including many of the earners of the biggest incomes.

Another recent change has been in the growth of self-employment. During the 1980s the number of people working for themselves, and not as employees, rose by half, from two million to almost three million, or more than one-tenth of the whole working population. This development was encouraged by the government, through training courses, tax incentives and an 'enterprise allowance scheme' under which people who have been unemployed may receive an allowance of £40 a week for the first year of running their own business.

2 Unemployment

The growth of the service and new manufacturing industries was not enough to prevent a high level of unemployment in the 1980s. After more than twenty years in which the unemployment rate was between 1 and 2 per cent, there was a big increase after 1974, to 6 per cent when Mrs Thatcher became Prime Minister in 1979. The rate then doubled in the next five years, and was around 12 per cent in 1984–86. It then fell slowly, to 6 per cent in 1990, though it then began to rise again. At most times about a third of the people registered as unemployed have been without jobs for a year or more; and at least a quarter of those currently working have recently been unemployed at some time. Most people have less job security than in the past.

There have always been big differences in the rates of unemployment in the various regions of the country. The areas with the highest unemployment are those which have been most dependent on the older manufacturing industries. But there are big differences within the regions too, with, for example, an unemployment rate five times greater in central parts of London and Manchester than in their more prosperous outer suburbs. But the recession which began in 1990 brought a change. Although the South-east's population, for the first time, had decreased, unemployment grew more quickly there than in the North.

All through this period of high unemployment the British addiction to overtime working has survived. The standard working week in industry is thirty-nine hours, but so much overtime is worked, at extra pay, that the average actual working week for full-time employees is more than forty-two hours, well above the European average.

Although there are now about eleven million women in the labour force (compared with seven million in the time of full employment in the 1950s), unemployment has consistently been at a lower rate among women than among men. One probable explanation for this difference is that women work mainly in the growing service industries.

3   Trade Unions

The Trades Union Congress is a single nationwide organisation with about eighty unions affiliated to it, and a total union membership of nine million (three million less than in 1979). Twenty of the unions have over 100,000 members each, but about fifty are very small.

Most unions are affiliated to the Labour Party, and hand over to the Party a small part of their members' subscriptions (though individual members may 'contract out' of the political levy). Only a few members take any interest in union affairs, or attend meetings, so power is in the hands of the enthusiasts. Each big union has a hierarchy of elected officers, central and local, and in many cases the union's national committee decides the main aspects of policy on behalf of the general membership. One of the main powers of these union bodies is to decide how to vote at the annual Labour Party conferences, not only on questions of party policy but also on the choice of the unions' members of the Party's National Executive Committee. More than a third of the Labour MPs are sponsored by one or another of eight big unions, and about a dozen other unions have one or more sponsored MPs to represent their interests in the House of Commons and the Parliamentary Labour Party.

Long before the 1980s the leaders of the biggest unions were commonly described, in medieval terms, as barons, great men of power without whose permission nothing new could be done. In 1973–74 Mr Heath's Conservative government tried to restrain inflation by setting limits to wage increases. The miners' union demanded more, then went on strike, and Mr Heath tried to assert his authority by calling a general election at a time when lack of electric power was causing regular power cuts and a three-day working week. Labour won that election and ruled in close partnership with the unions. After five years the partnership broke down. A series of strikes produced a 'winter of discontent', and at the end of it the Conservatives won their big majority in the 1979 election.

In the decades before the 1980s, even when unemployment was below 2 per cent, some unions, fearing job losses, resisted managements' attempts to modernise productive processes or to make full and profitable use of labour-saving equipment. At one time many of the strikes arose out of problems of demarcation between jobs or disputes between unions. A strike called by one union could stop a whole production line.

In the 1980s new laws set limits to union leaders' powers and privileges. Union officials must be elected for periods of no more than five years. New protection was given to workers not joining unions or expelled from them. Now, by law, strikes have to be approved by majorities of the workers affected, voting by secret ballot, and only six pickets can stand outside an entrance to a work place. The pickets must not be outsiders, and they must not behave in a threatening way.

Meanwhile, the new government policy left firms to compete for orders. Those who failed received no subsidy or protection. Some went out of business, some had to lay off workers. There was reason to fear unemployment. Most union leaders and shop stewards were soon accepting changes in work practices which they would have rejected a few years before.

During the 1980s the number of work days lost through strikes declined to a small proportion of the previous long-term average. Nearly all the big strikes of the past had ended with large concessions to the unions' demands. The few major strikes of the 1980s failed, though two of them were supported by mass-picketing which led to unprecedented clashes with the police who had been brought in to protect people still going to work. The miners' strike of 1984 failed to achieve its aim, to stop the closure of many uneconomic pits; and a section of the union, which opposed the strike, broke away to form a separate union. The newspaper printers' strike of 1986–87 failed because other unions collaborated with the management in bringing into operation a new process which did not need the printers. Later the Electrical, Electronic, Telecommunications and Plumbing Union, which had helped the management in this affair, was expelled from the TUC for its support for single-union agreements.

One feature of the past few decades has been the rise of white-collar unions, which now account for about a third of all unions, with a third of the total membership. Little more than a quarter of all working people are in manual jobs and union members, so the traditional unionised 'working class' is a minority of all workers. But the biggest 'white-collar' unions are associated particularly with public sector jobs. The late 1980s have produced cases of industrial action among hospital staffs and teachers, as well as postal and railway workers and prison officers. But workers in private sector industry have been more inclined to accept the needs of profitable business.

4 Changing Priorities

Before Mrs Thatcher's government came to power in 1979, both parties when in office had pursued many of the same objectives. They had given high priority to state action to keep unemployment at a low level. Firms had been given incentives to build their new factories at places chosen for social reasons. The direction of the economy had been planned jointly by ministers, representatives of industry and trade union leaders. Wages and prices had been controlled, sometimes with special limits on the increases of higher salaries. Taxation was used to reduce inequality; anyone who earned more than five times the average wage paid four-fifths of the top part of his earnings in income tax – and taxes on big 'unearned' incomes were higher still.

By the middle 1970s it was clear that this economic system had not been working well. By the main measure of success, 'per capita GNP' (the value of the nation's production of goods and services per person), Britain had progressed more slowly than any other major industrial country. West Germany had progressed much further, and France and several smaller countries had also overtaken Britain.

Mrs Thatcher's government came into office in 1979 with an aim to reverse Britain's relative economic decline by some fundamental changes in national economic policy. The state should be less involved in the economy. There should be more incentives for effort, more rewards for success, less protection for the unsuccessful; it was more important to use labour effectively than to aim at full employment. The power of the trade unions should be reduced. By 1989 big sections of the state-owned economy had been sold to the private sector (the telephone service and the gas and water industries) and were mostly making substantial and increasing profits. The generation and supply of electricity was privatised in 1990 and more 'privatisations' were being prepared.

By the later 1980s it could reasonably be claimed that the nation's relative economic decline had been reversed. In 1984–88 per capita GNP rose faster than in any other Western European country. The productivity of each worker had increased at a higher rate than in most other Western European countries – and in 1987 this increase even equalled that in Japan. By 1989 there was less unemployment than in many other countries in Western Europe. Although income tax had been steadily reduced, the state budget was in surplus.

The tax cuts within a balanced budget were made possible by the rise in personal incomes and company profits, and helped by profits from the oil of the North Sea. But government expenditure has remained at about two-fifths of the gross national product. Military defence has continued to cost more than in any other Western European country, partly because Britain maintains its own nuclear weapons, partly because some overseas commitments still survive from the imperial past, with the Falkland (or Malvinas) Islands adding their part to the total costs. The cost of law enforcement, including police, courts and prisons, has risen enormously in real terms. The high cost of all kinds of social services cannot easily be reduced when so many people are unemployed, the number of retired people is growing, and new and expensive forms of medical treatment make the health service more expensive. The Government's attempts to economise on these services, and on education, roads and other public works, have been bitterly criticised, particularly as taxes have been reduced. There is evidence that most people would prefer better public services even if they had to pay more taxes.

For people who have jobs, except the lowest paid, material conditions have improved as the result of higher purchasing power, with cars, good heating in their homes, machines in their kitchens, and holidays abroad. But there is less security at work and more fear of crime and illness.

One big change in the ownership of privately owned industry had begun long before the privatisations of the 1980s. Most private industry is run by big companies, many of them multinational, and for a long time more and more of their shares have been bought, not by individual people, but by institutions, mainly insurance companies and pension funds. The insurance companies use money entrusted to them by individuals in 'life' policies to provide them with income in addition to their state pension when they retire from work; the pension funds do much the same thing, but some are operated by firms on behalf of their employees, others by trade unions on behalf of their own members.

After 1980 the life insurance and pension funds grew even faster than before. Now they own between half and two-thirds of most big companies. Other institutions – investment trusts, local government councils and innumerable public bodies – are also important share owners. Some institutions also own big assets outside Britain, including real estate (such as office blocks in America) and shares in foreign companies; and probably a tenth of all British business is owned by foreign institutions. In many big companies the chairmen and directors together own less than one-thousandth of the shares. Ownership and control are rarely in the same hands – mainly in new or small companies.

The privatisations of the 1980s increased the number of people owning shares in companies. When an industry was sold off by the state, any person could buy a small block of shares. The price was set below the assessed value, so it seemed wise to buy. In 1987, when the aero-engine maker Rolls Royce was sold, two million people bought shares in the company. Within a year half of them had sold their shares at a profit, mainly to institutions. But, as with the telephone company and the gas industry, many small buyers have kept their shares. Meanwhile, older private-sector companies, as well as those sold by the state, make it advantageous for their own employees, at every level, to own shares in the businesses for which they work.

By 1988 three times as many people as ten years before owned shares in companies. A quarter of the adult population were individual share-holders. But this new spread of capitalist ownership has had an almost negligible effect on the overall shape of capitalism. It has still left the institutions as the major owners, and indirect public participation in ownership through the institutions is still the most significant element in the system. Through this system nearly everyone effectively owns some capital in private sector business.

A major objective of the policies of the 1980s has been to promote efficiency through competition. The earnings of the higher-paid have increased at a higher rate than those of the average employees, and the difference in spending power has been made greater still by the big reductions in the highest rate of income tax. This rapid increase of inequality has left many of the people in the lowest income groups worse off than they were before 1979.

By 1989 there were signs that the apparent new prosperity was insecure. The increase in real GNP per person overall had been no more in the ten years 1979–89 than in comparable earlier ten-year periods. Several opinions polls of the spring of 1989 found that most people were unenthusiastic about the recent economic changes. The collapse of share prices on the stock exchange in October 1987 had a disturbing parallel with the almost exactly similar collapse of 1929, which turned out to be the first warning stage of the great depression of the 1930s. The worldwide collapse of 1987 was attributed mainly to the trade and budget deficits of the United States, but by 1988–90 Britain's trade deficit was about the same as the United States on a per capita basis. Wages had risen at a rate faster than that which the rise in productivity would have justified. With lower taxes to pay on their bigger incomes, people were spending too much, particularly on imported goods and foreign holidays – and much of the expenditure was financed by borrowing. Inflation rose to an annual rate of over 10 per cent in 1990. A series of increases in interest rates cut the spending power of borrowers, particularly house-owners paying interest on their mortgages, and the rise in house prices in the south was checked. Within a few months the optimism of 1987 was replaced by a general pessimism about the economic prospects for 1989 and after.

Questions

TABLE 6.1

Changes in types of work people do
(thousands)

		1979	1983	1987	% change 1979–87
Production industries including agriculture, mining, power	Employees	9,494	7,568	7,053	− 25
	Self-employed	769	886	970	+ 30
Services ancillary to production including transport and distribution	Employees	4,773	4,506	4,698	− 1
	Self-employed	450	500	550	+ 12
Other services (education, health, catering, public administration, finance, etc.)	Employees	8,788	9,160	10,151	+ 18
	Self-employed	675	920	1,100	+ 65

TABLE 6.2

Employment and self-employment
(millions)

	1979	1983	1987	% change 1979–87
People working as employees	23.2	21.1	21.8	−6
Self-employed	2.0	2.6	2.6	+30

1   What do you think are the causes and implications of the switch in work from 'production' industries to 'services'?

2   Bearing in mind that many self-employed people are also employers, what do you think about the increase in self-employment?

3   In 1977 the chief of one of the biggest trade unions said on television, 'The interests of capital and labour are irreconcilable'.
    What factors in the modern British economy are relevant to an evaluation of this statement?

4   It is claimed that economic activity is more efficient if carried on by the private sector than by the public. Is this true?

TABLE 6.3

Average gain in income 1979 - 89

by tenths of the population. Effect after tax, social security changes.

(From The Institute of Fiscal Studies, published in *The Independent*, 13 May 1989)

TABLE 6.4

Changes in real earnings (corrected for inflation) of male employees and self-employed
(per cent)

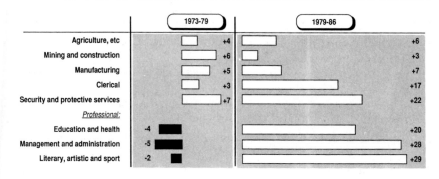

	1973-79	1979-86
Agriculture, etc	+4	+6
Mining and construction	+6	+3
Manufacturing	+5	+7
Clerical	+3	+17
Security and protective services	+7	+22
Professional:		
Education and health	-4	+20
Management and administration	-5	+28
Literary, artistic and sport	-2	+29

5 Discuss these figures in relation to:

a) the electoral success of the Thatcher government in 1982–87
b) the types of workers who have done best in this period
c) the argument that this Government's policies have been socially divisive.

TABLE 6.5

Average hours actually worked by full-time male employees, 1987

	Manual	Non-manual
Normal basic hours	39.1 (hours)	37.2 (hours)
Per cent working under 36 hours	2.2	20.3
Per cent working 36–40 hours	42.6	57.3
40–44	16.2	9.3
44–48	14.7	4.8
48–52	9.6	2.2
over 52	14.7	3.0

(From *Social Trends*)

6 Comment on these figures, given that:

a) overtime work is paid at extra rates
b) In Britain overtime is most common among male manual workers, that is, the category among which total numbers employed have fallen most, and among which there is most unemployment.

British schoolchildren.

7

The Status of Women and Ethnic Minorities

1 Women

Women aged over thirty gained full political equality (after a fifty-year campaign) in 1918; the age-differential, as compared with men, was ended ten years later. Women's votes have been helpful to the Conservatives – until 1987. At all previous elections for which surveys were taken, slightly more women than men voted for them. In 1987 men's and women's party preferences were identical. It is impossible to guess how much this change was a response to Labour's active sympathy for feminist causes, how much it was a negative reaction to Mrs Thatcher's policies.

The proportion of women elected to the House of Commons remained below 5 per cent until 1983. The 1979 election put Mrs Thatcher into office as Prime Minister, but only nineteen women were elected out of 635 MPs – or less than 3 per cent, the smallest number for over twenty years.

In the 1980s the Labour Party, in opposition, began to identify itself with all groups who feel excluded from the 'Establishment'. It had a plan to create a Ministry for Women. For the 1987 general election 92 of the 633 constituency Labour Parties selected women as their candidates, and twenty-one of them were elected to the House of Commons – or one in twelve of all Labour MPs – a greater proportion than at any previous time. With seventeen Conservative women MPs and three of other parties the House of Commons had forty-one women members. But even this record number is under 7 per cent, well below the proportion in the European countries which use party-list proportional systems of election. Long-term experience with single-seat constituencies indicates that the voters have no prejudice against women as such, but that the party activists who choose a party's candidates in safe seats tend to choose candidates who correspond with the party image. Conservative committees in safe seats tend to prefer prosperous men of high social class, Labour committees prefer men with working-class backgrounds.

Although the Conservatives choose so few women as their candidates for House of Commons seats which they expect to win, women are very active in the affairs of the party as a whole. In all parties a higher proportion of women is elected to local councils than to the House of Commons, and many of them attain leading positions. For a long time it has been usual to include one or more women among the members of the royal commissions and other committees which governments set up from time to time to examine aspects of the national life and to make reports.

Women have for a long time been active in the organisations which have grown up to improve and protect the environment in which we live, both physical and social. Cross-national comparisons indicate that the partici-pation and influence of women in activities of this kind is higher in Britain than in the rest of Western Europe except Scandinavia.

There are now around ten million women in paid employment, instead of seven million forty years ago. At that time only half as many women as men were 'economically active' in the labour force; now the difference is quite small. But a survey in 1986 showed that women still do nine-tenths of all cooking, washing, ironing and cleaning in the home. Many women work part time. Those who work full time earn on average two-thirds as much as men; the difference has been reduced less since 1979 than in the previous twenty years. But there are fewer women involuntarily unemployed.

Jobs done mainly or wholly by women are paid at relatively low rates, perhaps because they are done by women whose bargaining powers have been relatively weak. Women work less overtime. In career-type jobs few women are promoted to the highest and best-paid jobs in the hierarchies – including those in the Civil Service. Hardly any women are directors, or even high-grade executives, in big companies – even those whose main task is to sell goods to women.

In education the proportion of the women teachers declines both with the pupils' age and with the seniority of the position. The great majority of class teachers in the primary schools are women, but less than a sixth of the teaching staff of universities; female heads of secondary schools are very few, female university professors fewer still. Nearly half of the unpaid Justices of the Peace are women, but only one in forty of the professional and well-paid high court and circuit judges. The first woman appeal judge was appointed in 1987. Although by 1989 the three most popular Sunday newspapers all had women as editors, no woman had been the editor of any of the ten main national daily papers.

This situation has not been much affected by the law against sex discrimination, which was passed in 1975, or by the Equal Opportunities

A business meeting. There are few women in management positions.

Commission, appointed to monitor the operation of that law, or by the National Women's Commission, another statutory body. But it may be improved in future by the great changes that have taken place in higher education. In 1960 a quarter of all university students were women. They lived in separate colleges or halls of residence. Now aged fifty, some are teachers, most have grown-up children but did not work while their children were young; only the most determined have developed their careers. In 1989 two-fifths of a much bigger number of university students were women, no longer segregated in the student-residences. Five or ten times as many women as thirty years ago are becoming lawyers or accountants. There are hardly any crèches for their small children – and a Minister for Women might indeed fight effectively in Cabinet to provide them – but the new women graduates of the 1980s and 1990s will probably soon change the balance of the sexes in the higher jobs.

2 Immigrants from Europe

The British have a long tradition of receiving immigrants from across the seas, including refugees from persecution or poverty. Three hundred years ago a few thousand Protestant refugees from religious persecution came from France and some other parts of Europe, but their descendants are by now no longer a distinct group. In the eighteenth century labourers from Ireland built the canals, until a later generation built the railways. When Irish people come to live in Great Britain they are not considered to be foreign, and it is calculated that nearly a million people now in Britain can be recognised as Irish in their origins. Some keep their Irish links alive; there are two newspaper shops in one West London street, both selling many copies of twenty local papers from different parts of Ireland.

The oldest definable ethnic group is Jewish. In numbers it is small. Depending on definitions there are 300,000–400,000 Jews in Britain, or well under 1 per cent of the whole population. Most British Jews are descended from people who came from Eastern Europe in the nineteenth century. Before then a small number of Sephardic Jews were well established in international trade and banking, and in the 1930s there were refugees from Nazi persecution, most of them highly educated.

Many Jews from all these groups have attained great eminence through their contributions to the arts and academic life. Those who were concerned with politics were mainly active on the left. From 1950 to 1979 there were always at least twenty-five Jewish Labour members of the House of Commons, though few of them were much concerned with Jewish interests. But by the 1970s more Jews were moving to the right in politics: in 1989 there were only seven Jewish Labour MPs as opposed to sixteen Conservative MPs, including several ministers.

The Jewish population is now declining slowly, as a result of mixed marriages. Some Jews keep a strong attachment to their religion and to their community. Many live in a middle-class area of North London (which includes Mrs Thatcher's constituency). But for most practical purposes they are no less assimilated with the general community than the people of every European country who have settled in Britain, both recently and long ago. Some of these too maintain elements of a distinct national identity, both formal and informal – particularly people of Italian origin. In big towns, Poles, Ukrainians and others have their own churches, mostly taken over from English congregations which had dwindled and could no longer maintain the buildings.

3   Immigrants from outside Europe

Like other northern European countries Britain has received large numbers of immigrants from the Third World, but in Britain's case they have come mostly from the Indian subcontinent or the Caribbean. There are now well over a million people whose origins were in the Indian subcontinent, and 600,000 from the Caribbean. The number of people with Commonwealth origins, including those from Africa and the Far East, is about 4 per cent of the whole population. The vast majority are in London and the big cities of the midlands, rather fewer in other regions – though there is a big Muslim Asian community in West Yorkshire. Restrictions on immigration from the Commonwealth were first imposed in the 1960s, and have been kept, with variations, since that time.

There are a few industrial areas where big Asian communities remain closely knit, with many of their people working in local factories. In one of these, Southall in West London, Sikhs and Hindus have reflected the conflict within India. In the West Yorkshire area there are many separate schools for those Muslims who want them. Some Muslims and Hindus at first arrived in Britain with English as their second language. Some came knowing no English, but equipped to work in factories along with others speaking the same language.

Many Asians work for public services and many others run their own businesses. Together with their Chinese competitors (kept mainly by people from Hong Kong), Indian restaurants provide a fine addition to the great variety of eating places available in most towns. Londoners and other city people also have good reason to be grateful to the Asians who have taken over many of the small shops. Typically these are run by families who keep them open late at night and on Sundays, and help to keep the streets alive in spite of the competition of the supermarkets.

There is by now a big Asian middle class, based on both business and the professions. In the 1960s some newly-independent Commonwealth countries in East Africa drove out the Indians who over the past few generations had established themselves as leaders of their commerce. Some brought their experience and skill to Britain, although they were discouraged by the Labour government then in power. It now seems that children of Indian origin are having a better success rate with secondary school examinations than the native British children.

For the immigrants from the Caribbean, coming from societies with many of their customs as well as their first language close to the British pattern, there was less fundamental novelty in the new homeland. But some were disappointed when they could not get jobs of the same status as

95

those they had left behind. In some respects the people from the Caribbean have had experiences similar to those of American blacks who have moved to northern cities of the United States, with high unemployment for unqualified young black people. People of West Indian origin have excelled in several forms of athletic sports, and Britain's most recent teams at Olympic Games have included many black people. The Caribbean influence on song and dance is obvious.

The House of Commons had two members of Indian origin elected in the 1890s, but none from 1929 to 1987. In the 1980s there was dissatisfaction at the continuing failure of local parties to choose black or Asian candidates for seats which a party could hope to win. A demand for the establishment of 'black sections' of the Labour Party (implying some kind of quota) was rejected by the leadership. However, at the election of 1987 four black or Asian Labour candidates were elected to the House of Commons. A further twenty-four candidates were defeated, twenty-two of them in constituencies the party could not hope to win. The Conservatives put up six black or Asian candidates, all in hopeless seats, and who were all defeated.

Questions

TABLE 7.1

Percentage of women with children working, 1987			
Age of youngest child	Mother working		Mother not working
	full time	part time	
0–5	9.7	22.6	67.6
5–10	15.5	44.4	40.0
10–15	25.1	44.6	30.0

1 Is the increasing tendency for mothers to go out to work good for their children?

2 Ought there to be more nursery schools and playgroups?
Should mothers using them pay all, or some, or none, of the cost of providing them?
Should they be available for (say) nine or ten hours a day?

3 Has the permissive society made life more satisfactory for women?

4   Now that the proportion of women with professional qualifications is increasing, do you expect to see more women in top positions in business and public administration?

5   In the past twenty years a woman, Laura Ashley, built up a business which has become famous and international. Why are so few women made directors of big established companies?

TABLE 7.2

Ethnic groups in Britain, 1988

Area of origin	Thousands	Percentage of population
West Indies	521	1.0
Africa	105	0.2
Indian sub-continent	1260	2.3
China (including Hong Kong)	120	0.2
Other	896	1.8

6   Considering that a third to a half of most of these groups were born in Britain, do you see the future mainly as an opportunity for assimilation, or for the development of a multicultural society, or for some other movement?

7   Can you explain the idea of a multicultural society?

Holidaymakers on the beach at Blackpool.

A country pub.

8

Leisure and Private Life

1 Holidays

Nearly all British people in full-time jobs have at least four weeks' holiday a year, often in two or three separate periods. The normal working week is 35–40 hours, Monday to Friday. People who have to work in shifts with 'unsocial' hours are paid extra for the inconvenience. More overtime is worked (at extra pay) than in most other Western European countries, but there is relatively little 'moonlighting' – that is, independent work for pay in leisure hours. (Another way of saying this is that the 'black economy', involving work paid privately in cash and not officially recorded or taxed, is relatively small.)

There are only eight official public holidays a year, only one of them in the six months before Christmas. None of them celebrates anything to do with state or nation, though the first Monday in May was made a 'bank holiday' (national holiday) by a recent Labour government as the British holiday in honour of working people.

The most obvious – and traditional – British holiday destination is the coast. No place in the country is more than three hours' journey from some part of it. The coast is full of variety, with good cliffs and rocks between the beaches, but the uncertain weather and cold sea are serious disadvantages. Also, two weeks in a hotel room with balcony and private bath can now cost less in Spain or Greece, with flight included, than the same in a British hotel. Most of the hotels in the numerous seaside resort towns were built in the railway age, between 50 and 100 years ago, and seem now to be used as much by people going to conferences as by those on holiday. Going to a conference can be a sort of holiday, even in working time and with expenses paid.

People who go for one or two weeks' holiday to the coast, or to a country place, tend now to take their caravans or tents to campsites, or rent static caravans, cottages or flats. Some take tents, but their optimism is usually disappointed. Many town dwellers have bought old country cottages, to use for their own holidays and to let to others when they are working themselves.

People on holiday or travelling around the country often stay at farms or other houses which provide 'bed and breakfast'. These are usually comfortable and better value than hotels.

By now the holiday resorts most popular with the British are on the Mediterranean coasts, or yet further south. In 1988 a third of all British people went abroad, mainly to places where warm sea and sunshine can be confidently expected. Most travel by air on 'package' holidays, paying for flight, local tax and hotel or flat all together, others travel by car or bus and ferry. If affluence continues to grow and spread more widely, it seems likely that foreign travel will grow more quickly still, particularly in winter to places not too far from the equator.

2 Sport

The British are great lovers of competitive sports; and when they are neither playing nor watching games they like to talk about them, or when they cannot do that, to think about them.

The game particularly associated with England is cricket. Many other games which are English in origin have been adopted with enthusiasm all over the world, but cricket has been seriously and extensively adopted only in the former British empire, particularly in Australia, New Zealand, India, Pakistan, Sri Lanka, the West Indies and South Africa.

Organised amateur cricket is played between club teams, mainly on Saturday afternoons. Nearly every village, except in the far north, has its cricket club, and there must be few places in which the popular image of England, as sentimentalists like to think of it, is so clearly seen as on a village cricket field. A first-class match between English counties lasts for up to three days, with six hours' play on each day. The game is slow, and a spectator, sitting in the afternoon sun after a lunch of sandwiches and beer, may be excused for having a little sleep for half an hour.

For the great mass of the British public the eight months of the football season are more important than the four months of cricket. There are plenty of amateur association football (or 'soccer') clubs, and professional football is big business. The annual Cup Final match, between the two teams which have defeated their opponents in each round of a knock-out contest, dominates the scene; the regular 'league' games, organised in four divisions, provide the main entertainment through the season and the basis for the vast system of betting on the football pools. Many of the graffiti on public walls are aggressive statements of support for football teams, and the hooliganism of some British supporters has become notorious outside as well as inside Britain.

Rugby football (or 'rugger') is played with an egg-shaped ball, which may be carried and thrown (but not forward). If a player is carrying the ball he may be 'tackled' and made to fall down. Each team has fifteen players, who spend a lot of time lying in the mud or on top of each other and become very dirty, but do not need to wear such heavily protective clothing as players of American football. There is some professional Rugby League in the North, but elsewhere Rugby Union is played by amateurs and favoured by the middle-class. It is also the game played at most 'public schools', including Rugby itself, where it was invented. International matches, involving England, Wales, Scotland, Ireland and France, are played in capital cities with crowds of up to 80,000, but a match between two top clubs may be watched by only a few hundred spectators.

Most secondary schools have playing fields, and boys normally play rugger or soccer in winter and cricket in summer; girls play tennis and rounders (similar to baseball) in summer and netball and hockey in winter. Hockey is also becoming more and more popular at boys' schools, and there are many men's amateur hockey clubs. Men's basketball is played by a tiny minority.

Golf courses (together with the bars in their club houses) are popular meeting places of the business community; it is, for example, very desirable for bank managers to play golf. There are plenty of tennis clubs, but most towns provide tennis courts in public parks, and anyone may play tennis cheaply on a municipal court. There are cheap municipal golf courses in Scotland but few in England. The ancient game of bowls is played, much more sedately than in southern France, mainly by middle-aged people, on reserved level stretches of beautifully kept grass, often in municipal parks.

The biggest new development in sport has been with long-distance running. 'Jogging', for healthy outdoor exercise, needing no skill or equipment, became popular in the 1970s, and soon more and more people took it seriously. Now the annual London Marathon is like a carnival, with a million people watching as the world's star runners are followed by 25,000 ordinary people trying to complete the course. Most of them succeed and then collect money from supporters for charitable causes. Many thousands of people take part in local marathons all over Britain.

The first fully organised Olympic Games of the modern era were held in London in 1908, and every Olympic sport has its practitioners in

101

Britain. For a long time now British teams have not won many medals. After many years of complaints that governments had not provided enough resources, or material encouragement, Prime Minister Wilson appointed a Minister for Sport in 1974. This post has often been held by a politician with a sporting background – in 1988 by a former rowing star.

Rowing is one Olympic sport which has a great history in Britain, beginning in some schools and universities. Some regattas on the Thames have been spectacular social events for well over a hundred years, and today's best rowers have had international successes. But with dozens of other sports, including gymnastics, large resources, and hence money, are needed to encourage popular participation to discover talent and develop its potential. Although plenty of new sports centres have been built, they have difficulty in competing for an adequate share of public expenditure. In the conditions of the 1980s some local authorities had to close public swimming pools.

Cycling is a fairly popular pastime, but few people take it up as a serious sport, and it is not a very popular spectator sport. Sailing and horseriding are popular among those who can afford them, and some yacht races attract wider interest, particularly the regattas off Cowes, in the waters sheltered by the Isle of Wight.

Horse racing is big business, along with the betting which sustains it. Every day of the year, except Sundays, there is a race meeting at at least one of Britain's several dozen racecourses. Nine-tenths of the betting is done by people all over the country, by post or at local betting shops, and it is estimated that a tenth of all British men bet regularly on horse races, many of them never going to a race course.

Greyhound racing has had a remarkable revival in the 1980s, and by 1988 it accounted for about a quarter of all gambling. Its stadiums are near town centres, small enough to be floodlit in the evenings. Until recently the spectators were mostly male and poor, the surroundings shabby. The 1980s have changed all this, with the growth of commercial sponsorship for advertising. There are fewer stadiums and fewer spectators than in 1970, but the old cloth cap image has become much less appropriate. But one thing has not changed. The élite of Britain's dogs, and their trainers, mostly come from Ireland.

Horse racing accounts for about half of all gambling, dog racing for a quarter (after increasing by 27 per cent in 1987–88). The total gambling expenditure is estimated at over three billion pounds a year, or nearly 1 per cent of the gross domestic product – though those who bet get about three-quarters of their stake back in winnings. There is no national lottery, though premium bonds are a form of national savings, with monthly prizes instead of interest. About half of all households bet regularly on the football pools, although half of the money staked is divided between the state, through taxes, and the operators. People are attracted by the hope of winning huge prizes, but some winners become miserable with their sudden unaccustomed wealth. Bingo sessions, often in old cinemas, are attractive mainly to women, and have a good social element. More popular are the slot machines in establishments described as 'amusement arcades'. There has been some worry about the addiction of young people to this form of gambling, which can lead to theft.

The most popular of all outdoor sports is fishing, from the banks of lakes or rivers or in the sea, from jetties, rocks or beaches. Some British lakes and rivers are famous for their trout or salmon, and attract enthusiasts from all over the world.

The British do not shoot small animals or birds for sport, though some farmers who shoot rabbits or pigeons may enjoy doing so. But 'game birds', mainly pheasant, grouse and partridge, have traditionally provided sport for the landowning gentry.

Until Labour's election victory of 1964 many of the prime ministers of the past two hundred years, along with members of their cabinets, had gone to the grouse moors of Scotland or the Pennines for the opening of the shooting season on 12 August. Since 1964 all that has changed. Now there are not many leading British politicians carrying guns in the shooting parties, though there may be foreign millionaires, not all of them from America. Some of the beaters, whose job is to disturb the grouse so that they fly up to be shot, are students earning money to pay for trips abroad. But there is still a race to send the first shot grouse to London restaurants, where there are people happy to pay huge amounts of money for the privilege of eating them.

Another sport, also associated through the centuries with ownership of land, is the hunting of foxes. The hounds chase the fox, followed by people riding horses, wearing red or black coats and conforming with various rules and customs. In a few hill areas stags are hunted similarly. Both these types of hunting are enjoyed mainly by people who can afford the cost of keeping horses and carrying them to hunt meetings in 'horse boxes', or trailer vans. Both, particularly stag-hunting, are opposed by people who condemn the cruelty involved in chasing and killing frightened animals. There have been attempts to persuade Parliament to pass laws to forbid hunting, but none has been successful.

3   Theatre and Cinema

London has several dozen theatres, most of them not far from Trafalgar Square. A successful play can run for many months or even years. Outside London some quite big towns have no public theatre at all, and hardly any towns have more than three. But there are private theatres, some attached to colleges or schools. Innumerable amateur groups produce plays, often with some professional help, in these theatres which they hire or borrow, or in halls temporarily equipped with makeshift stage furniture. Shakespeare is honoured by a great modern theatre in the small town of Stratford-upon-Avon, where he was born. But serious theatre needs subsidy to survive.

Several first-rate orchestras are based in London. The largest provincial centres also maintain permanent orchestras, which give regular concerts. All these orchestras occasionally visit other places to give concerts, and some financial help is given to them by the Arts Council or by local authorities. The Royal Opera House at Covent Garden, in central London, is leased by the government to the Covent Garden Opera House Trust, which receives a government grant. Seasons of opera are performed there and also of ballet by the Royal Ballet, which has in recent years been one of the most successful of British ventures in the arts.

Touring opera and ballet companies visit the principal theatres in major towns. Opera of the highest quality is performed throughout every summer in Glyndebourne, 90 kilometres south of London but visited by people who come from London and its suburbs.

Local enterprise has been responsible for the development in recent years of 'festivals' of the arts in several places, of which the best known is the annual International Festival of Music and Drama in Edinburgh, held in late August. As well as the performances by musicians, etc. from all over the world, the 'fringes' of the Festival produce an interesting variety of plays by less established companies. Among other such festivals are those held at Bath, Aldeburgh (connected with the composer Benjamin Britten), Pitlochry in the Scottish Highlands and Llangollen in north-central Wales. The Three Choirs Festival, which circulates among the three western cathedral cities of Gloucester, Worcester and Hereford, has a continuous history going back to 1724.

British governments have been less generous than many others with subsidies to serious or experimental drama, music and ballet. There is a Minister for the Arts (not a member of the Cabinet) and an Arts Council which receives a grant from the government (£194 million in 1991–2). Part of this money is used to sustain the performing arts, but it is easy to complain that some performances are helped which do not deserve such help. The whole question of subsidy to the arts creates a dilemma for politicians dedicated to the market, and reluctant to use tax revenues to support the expensive enjoyments of minorities, however worthy. Yet they do not wish to be accused of philistinism. Meanwhile, some big companies are helping by sponsoring performances.

From about 1930 until quite recent times the cinema enjoyed an immense popularity, and the large cinemas built in the 1930s were the most impressive of the buildings to be seen in the streets of many towns. More recently the rapid spread of television has brought a great change. In 1946 the average British person went to the cinema forty times a year, but by the 1980s the figure had fallen to 1.2 times, and 1,500 cinemas were closed during this period. Most films shown are from Hollywood, but some British films have won great international success. For foreign-language films there is a healthy prejudice against 'dubbed' English soundtracks, and such films are usually shown with English subtitles.

Censorship of the theatre 'for the preservation of good manners, decorum and the public peace' was at last abolished in 1968, but some films are classified as unsuitable for children. More than half of all households have video equipment, sometimes used for viewing films on the home TV set. Video-film hiring is big business.

4   Other Recreations

Visitors to provincial England sometimes find the lack of public activities in the evenings depressing. There are, however, many activities which visitors do not see. Evening classes, each meeting once a week, are flourishing immensely, and not only those which prepare people for examinations leading to professional qualifications. Many people attend classes connected with their hobbies, such as photography, painting, folk dancing, dog training, cake decoration, archaeology, local history, car maintenance and other subjects. Classes may be organised by local education authorities or by bodies like the Workers' Educational Association, and in them people find an agreeable social life as well as the means of pursuing their own hobbies. All this, together with the popularity of amateur dramatics, can provide some comfort for those who fear that modern mass entertainment is producing a passive society.

Other groups meet regularly for a mixture of social and religious purposes or for the pursuit of hobbies. For young people there are youth clubs, some, but not all, of them connected with churches.

Young and old spend leisure time working together for good causes, raising money for the benefit of victims of famine, flood or misfortune. All of this demands a good deal of organisation and innumerable committees. Most of it needs money, and the workers for charities spend much time in trying to extract funds from the rest of the community to supplement the subscriptions which they pay themselves. Subject to the regulations made by the public authorities and with their permission, the supporters of a charity may organise a 'flag-day', normally not more than once a year in any town. They stand in the streets with collecting boxes into which generously disposed passers-by put money, receiving in exchange little paper 'flags' to pin on their coats. Other devices are 'bazaars' or 'sales of work', where home made food and unwanted clothes are sold, and opening speeches are made by persons of importance. All these activities turn out to be social occasions. In the course of doing good the public-spirited develop their social lives, meet their friends and enjoy themselves.

Public libraries, maintained by the local authorities, are well developed and progressive, and everywhere allow people to borrow books without charge. The books in the lending section are always kept on open shelves, and library staffs are very helpful in getting books on request from other libraries through the exchange system. Most libraries report an increase in borrowing over the past few years, so television does not seem to be stopping people from reading, as it was feared that it would. Many towns have well and imaginatively kept museums and art galleries, with no charge for admission at least until 1990. By then some of the national museums were charging for admission.

England is famous for its gardens, and most people like gardening. This is probably one reason why so many people prefer to live in houses rather than in flats. Particularly in suburban areas it is possible to pass row after row of ordinary small houses, each one with its neatly kept patch of grass surrounded by a great variety of flowers and shrubs. Some people who have no garden of their own have patches of land or 'allotments' in special areas. Enthusiasts of gardening – or do-it-yourself activities – get ever-growing help from radio programmes, magazines and patient shop-keepers.

Although the task of keeping a garden is essentially individual, gardening can well become the foundation of social and competitive relationships. Flower shows and vegetable shows, with prizes for the best exhibits, are popular, and to many gardeners the process of growing the plants seems more important than the merely aesthetic pleasure of looking at the flowers or eating the vegetables.

Two traditional British institutions, the pub and fish-and-chip shop, have been transformed in the past two or three decades. A few pubs still have gloomy walls and frosted-glass windows, ugly bars where people drink standing up. But in most of today's pubs, although the customers still buy their drinks at the bar, they usually carry them away to sit comfortably at tables in an ambience both civilised and aesthetically pleasing. Many pubs have tables outside, sometimes in well-tended gardens, with swings for children. Many of them provide food, not only sandwiches but salads and hot dishes, often very good and usually good value. The opening hours were liberalised at last in 1988, allowing pubs to stay open all day. However, some still keep to the old practice, so long imposed by law, of closing for about three hours in the afternoon. Although a lot of trouble is caused by people who get drunk, mostly at weekends, the British drink less alcohol than most other Europeans. They now drink less beer but more wine than in the past.

Fish-and-chip shops no longer wrap up their wares in newspapers, to be eaten in the street outside, but provide more commodious containers. Most offer chicken or sausages too, or quite often Chinese dishes. Some indeed are run by people who came originally from China or Hong Kong. They have their rivals like hamburger and fried chicken bars. And most of the ubiquitous Indian and Chinese restaurants are prepared to put their rice and curry, or their noodle dishes, in little boxes to take away. But these are serious meals, with twenty minutes' preparation time, so take-away customers can avoid delay by telephoning in advance.

For eating out in towns there is a marvellous variety of choice. Many of the Indian restaurants are very good indeed. Other restaurants are of several different nationalities, some providing simple dishes, some more ambitious. British people eat out in restaurants or hotel dining rooms more now than in the past, not only for conferences, business or club meetings, but as a family activity.

There is a strong tradition of hospitality, and most entertaining in people's homes is free and easy, informal, and without rituals. The old afternoon tea party has lost popularity, even on Sunday, partly because few people dare to eat the fattening scones, butter and jam and cakes which go with the traditional English tea. Instead, friends and relations are asked for drinks before lunch or dinner, or for a meal which nowadays is sometimes a buffet supper eaten away from the table.

5   Marriage, Home and Family

The mid-twentieth century has brought three great and obvious changes to family life: contraception, personal mobility, and a concern for the equality of women. Along with these, and linking them, we have a value system which rejects the idea that anyone is superior to anyone else, and hence a rejection of established authority except that which arises within a self-conscious peer-group. Old accepted patterns of behaviour, including courtship and the ways by which men and women meet, have disappeared, and have been replaced by nothing definable.

At home most parents do not restrict the movements of their children, in particular their daughters, as much as they used to. Girls expect to go to work when they finish their education, no matter at what age between sixteen and twenty-three. They meet men at work, within their peer group and through their friends. Some form stable relationships early, others have several relationships in succession. Most young people have sex before marriage. Most are successful in avoiding unwanted pregnancy at this stage, some marry if pregnancy does occur. Increasing numbers of couples set up home without being married.

For those who become pregnant and are unable or unwilling to marry, abortion has been available, subject to restrictions, since 1967. The restrictions are not very precise, and their meaning depends mainly on the interpretations of individual medical practitioners. Even so, the number of legal abortions carried out in any year has not exceeded 160,000. The main effect of the easing of the law has been to reduce enormously the incidence of bad effects on the health of women. A large proportion of abortions are performed on married women who already have several children.

In one way the new acceptance of extra-marital sexual activity has been bad for women; it is easier for men to avoid responsibility, and in a world where people are encouraged to think that they have a right to whatever they want, some women suffer from being treated without the personal respect which older values expected men to show.

Most women who marry continue to go out to work until they have children, and few have more than two children. The birth rate declined in 1965–77 as in most other countries, and in 1987 was around the EEC average at 13 per 1,000 population.

Most women with very small children stay at home to look after them, unless they can make other arrangements. Few married couples live near to their own parents, and grandparents are likely to go out to work themselves. There are not enough places in nursery schools to provide for all the mothers who would like to go to work, but a few workplaces provide crèches, and children can be left with private 'childminders' registered with the local authorities.

Parents have become more indulgent to their children in every way, giving them more presents and money and not exercising much discipline. There is so much variety that generalisation is unwise, but serious misbehaviour, including vandalism, by young children, increased ten times over in twenty years, and is often blamed on weak parental control. The 'problem families' are well known to the huge army of social service workers.

In well-adjusted families modern life gives scope for more collective family activity, which is helped by owning a car and garden. Improved housing has made family life more private, and with privacy has gone a decline in the informal social control of neighbours' opinions. While the nuclear family of parents and children has grown closer together (except where the children demand and take more independence), the extended family has become weaker. Young people, when they marry, tend to live well away from their parents and other relations, often in different towns; and many people in non-manual careers move from one town to another at intervals of five, ten or fifteen years, so that many children hardly know their aunts, uncles or cousins.

Whatever the reason, the nuclear family as an institution has not universally adapted itself to these recent changes. Until 1971 divorce was obtainable without much difficulty on the ground of 'matrimonial offence', but then a new law allowed divorce by agreement, defined as 'irretrievable breakdown of marriage'. When married people have difficulties they may ask for help and advice from the unpaid counsellors of a private organisation, the former Marriage Guidance Council, now called 'Relate'. In spite of these efforts, the divorce rate doubled in ten years, and is now the highest in any Western European country. About a third of all marriages end in divorce, and a much smaller number in legal separation. The legal costs involved in divorce and separation may be substantial, but are often funded from the legal aid system, paid out of tax revenue. Meanwhile the number of couples who set up home together without marrying has increased enormously.

The legal arrangements for a divorce or separation normally require the father to pay a weekly allowance to the mother, but not all fathers keep up their payments. Magistrates' courts spend much time trying to put pressure on defaulting fathers, but the ultimate sanction, prison, does not help anyone. Many children of divorced parents, as well as those of unmarried mothers, depend on social security payments for their support, and some of them also need help from the local authorities' social services.

The word 'permissiveness' is used to describe a characteristic of modern times. The laws allow actions which were once forbidden, and when people break the laws every effort is made to treat them as victims of circumstances rather than as people deserving anger and punishment. Meanwhile the old social controls of religion, extended family and close-knit neighbourhood have been weakened. The new freedoms, along with the newly-available material goods, have created opportunities for freer and more varied living; and where they produce misery (for example, among the victims of individual anti-social acts) the public authorities have a vast and caring apparatus through which to help. Professional social workers have to make difficult decisions – for example when to recommend that their local authority should take into its care children who are neglected or ill-treated by their parents. Children in care are often sent to live with other families who then act as foster parents. Some decisions have gone wrong, and the damage and distress caused by such errors has done some harm to public confidence in the official social services.

Questions

TABLE 8.1

Annual household expenditure on some leisure items

| | Household income per year | | |
	Under £5,000	Over £15,000	Average income
Meals out	£50	£500	£220
Drinks out	£80	£550	£300
Books, newspapers, etc.	£70	£220	£130
Holidays	£35	£650	£280
Admissions and entertainments	£20	£250	£100
All leisure as percentage of total expenditure	8%	55%	29%

1 What do you consider the most significant aspects of these figures?

2 Compare these two opinions
   a) In a civilised society sports facilities, museums and libraries should be paid for out of taxation, on a generous scale and with long hours of opening.

b) People who do not use sports facilities, museums and libraries should not have to pay for those who do use them.

3 Why do you think that Britain has no national lottery?

4 The number of divorces each year in the UK grew sevenfold in twenty years, 1961–81, to about 50 per cent above the French and West German rates, and ten times the Italian.

In the 1980s the rate of divorce in the UK did not change much. In most years there were about:

250,000 marriages of people previously not married
130,000 marriages with one or both partners divorced
150,000 divorces

With the divorce rate stabilised in the 1980s, the number of people living together unmarried doubled in 1981–87. In 1987 one child in six was born to unmarried couples who registered the births jointly, as though they were married, and one child in fifteen was born to a single mother.

By 1987 one child in seven was living with a single parent.

Does it seem that the family as an institution is becoming old-fashioned?

5 About two-fifths of single-parent households have disposable incomes per person of less than half the national average. The single-parent situation seems to be a much more prevalent cause of poverty in Britain, the USA and elsewhere, than old age, illness or unemployment. What should be done about this growing problem?

TABLE 8.2

Changing opinions about sexual morality

	Percentage saying it is wrong
Couples living together when not married	14
Having a child outside marriage (only 7% of respondents aged under 24, but 44% of those over 65, thought this wrong)	23
Adultery by married people	51

(From the MORI opinion poll, reported in *The Sunday Times*, 8 January 1989)

6 What do the figures imply for the role of the traditional family in modern society?

*A suburban
housing estate.*

Council housing in London.

9

Houses, Cars and Public Transport

1 Planning and the Environment

In the 1970s the counties of Britain prepared new long-term structure plans for their development, based on forecasts of population, industry and services, with zones designated for residence or business or preserved open space. There were innumerable public meetings where elected councillors and officials answered questions from the thousands of citizens who had studied the plans and wanted to hear explanations or to suggest changes. The local councils' plans were then submitted to the central government, which could modify them.

This process was based on the idea that government should work hard to improve the physical environment, with local plans coordinated to conform with central policy. But by the 1980s there was some loss of confidence in the ability of any government to achieve such rational objectives. Mrs Thatcher had more faith in market forces than in ambitious comprehensive planning; instead of trying to do more, government should do less.

2 Housing

English people traditionally prefer to live in houses with their own front doors, preferably with gardens behind and better still with front gardens too. The streets built in the nineteenth century had very few apartment blocks. Except in places where stone is easily available, the usual building material is red brick, sometimes covered with stucco or rough-cast material. Until about 1910 most town houses were built in terraces on two, three or four floors, with each level having one room at the front, one at the back, and space for hall and stairs. The more opulent houses were detached or built in pairs, with space to the side as well.

Scotland's housing history is different, more like most of continental

Europe, with tenement buildings and bare stone stairs climbing up to flats at the upper levels.

The divisions between the social classes have always been reflected in the geography of towns, with the bigger and better houses concentrated in the most salubrious districts. The process began before 1800, and the Georgian terraces which survive have been particularly admired all through the past fifty years. The much more decorated houses of the late nineteenth century, though less elegant, have come back into fashion. In many cases the 'nice' parts of towns would be on the west, because the prevailing south-west wind blew the smoke from the coal-burning fires towards the east. In such areas many single-family houses, both Georgian and Victorian, had four or five floors, with basements and top floors kept for servants and the children and their nannies. Today many houses of this kind have been divided into 'maisonettes' of two floors each, or into flats which are useful to the growing number of one-person households, or to students. The old middle-class status still survives, partly because the middle class is growing, as a proportion of the population as a whole. Indeed, some old 'working-class' areas, usually those nearby, are being 'gentrified'.

From the 1920s the outward spread of towns produced tidy rows of small houses, mostly built in pairs (semi-detached), and owned by their occupants with the help of mortgages from ordinary banks or housing loan banks, called building societies. Suburban building of this kind was stopped all through the 1940s, but has flourished since that time.

The period from 1945 produced a huge growth of social housing, built by local authorities for letting at low rents with the help of central government subsidies. Some of this 'council housing' has been on town fringes, mainly at low densities. Most old town terrace houses belonged to private landlords, many of whom were poor themselves. Rents were fixed by law at levels too low to leave money to pay for maintenance. By 1950 whole streets were damp, rotten and condemned as unfit for habitation. During the next twenty years there was large-scale demolition of old town housing, and local councils used the land to build blocks of flats, first up to about five storeys, then, for a few years, in towers of fifteen, twenty or more storeys.

This great change from traditional English housing patterns was seen as a triumph of modern planning and technology. Instead of cramped streets, the new tower blocks had space around them. With modern methods they were built quite cheaply, yet to high standards of interior space and comfort, and the upper flats had good views. But by the 1970s things were going wrong. Families with children were placed in high-up flats, and did not like them. The entrances were not supervised. There was vandalism, robbery and violence, litter and graffiti. Lifts were damaged. Then it turned out that there were some serious deficiencies in construction. The tower blocks became the object of a whole vocabulary of insults, and after about 1970 no more were built by local councils.

These bad experiences did some harm to the reputation of the councils as house-owners and as planners of land use. At the same time a higher value was placed on the old terraces built in the days before the rise of the bureaucrats and planners. As tenants with controlled rents died or went away, landlords sold their houses in the open market, not to new landlords but to people who became owner-occupiers and revived these run-down properties.

By 1979 Labour had been in power for nearly twelve out of fifteen years, and had continued to encourage council housing. Just over a third of all households were by then council tenants – more than at any previous time. Council tenants enjoyed security of tenure and low rents, even if they became prosperous. In 1980 it was estimated that a quarter of council-tenant households earned above average incomes – and were inclined to vote Labour, while home-owners with similar incomes were inclined to vote Conservative.

The newly-elected Thatcher government, with its firm commitment to the old Conservative ideal of a 'property-owning democracy' (including home-ownership) considered that this proportion was too high. They also thought that local councils, with political control and bureaucratic management, were not the right bodies to manage people's houses. Housing subsidies were reduced: in the 1980s the number of new houses built by local councils fell to a tenth of its former level. Councils were obliged to sell their houses to any tenants who wanted to buy them and could afford to do so. In ten years about a fifth of all council tenants bought their houses, mostly at between a third and two-thirds of their estimated open-market value, though they could not then sell them quickly at a profit.

Meanwhile, another form of tenure, through housing associations, was encouraged, with some new building and some transfer of council housing to this sector. New private building flourished. Local councils were discouraged from being too strict in refusing permission to build new houses on land outside designated building zones. By 1989 nearly two-thirds of householders owned their homes, though the variation between areas was enormous: above four-fifths in some parliamentary constituencies, below a tenth in others, mainly in some inner cities.

Meanwhile, private letting was encouraged, with rents for new tenancies able to be fixed at market rates for stipulated periods. The long-term decline of private tenancy, to just over a tenth of all households, slowed down.

But the most significant development with housing has been with the market price. For most of the past fifty years house prices have increased at a rate far above inflation, and the rise accelerated in the 1980s. In the London area the price of a typical terrace house built around 1900 rose, in 1950–88, from three times to ten times the annual average wage. The rest of south-east England saw nearly similar increases, and after 1987 the fastest rises were in some areas between 100 and 200 kilometres from London.

The situation created difficulties for first-time buyers too young to have accumulated savings. Also, with a house in the south-east costing two or three times as much as its equivalent in the north, it became difficult for people to move from north to south. However, in 1989–90 house prices fell, particularly in the south.

The new policies produced a big increase in the number of homeless people. By 1989 the London boroughs were accommodating 50,000 in bed-and-breakfast houses – nearly 1 per cent of London's population. But the majority of the people were living in their own houses, bought some time before and happy with the unexpected wealth which the vastly increased value of their houses had brought to them. Many people in their fifties, already owner-occupiers of good houses, can look forward to a retirement made prosperous by the sale of houses they inherit. Almost all the people are comfortably housed, except for some of the very old, and people living in vandalised council flats and houses. There are very few houses without proper heating or sanitation, and there is little overcrowding. The exceptions may be very bad, but they are also very few.

3   Cars and Roads

The British own slightly fewer cars than the people of West Germany, France or Italy: a little more than one for every three people. But there are big local variations. In some northern cities car ownership is low by modern standards, with less than one car for every two households; in some counties around London there are more cars than households.

In addition to value added tax on new cars, car owners pay a fixed rate annual car tax and a tax on fuel, all to central funds. About a quarter of what they pay is in fact spent on roads, the rest is a contribution to the general revenue, like taxes on alcohol and tobacco. The central government uses its funds to pay for the motorways and roads of national importance; counties pay for minor roads but get some grants from the central government to help with these local costs. The taxes are about equal to the Western European average, but expenditure rather less.

There are greater lengths of motorway in Benelux than in Britain, which has twice the population. France and Italy, with populations about equal to Britain's, have twice the length of motorway. Most British motorways have three lanes each side, and service stations with restaurants about fifty kilometres apart. There are no tolls, except for a few bridges and tunnels for which the tolls, particularly on lorries, are extremely low.

In addition to the 3,000 kilometres of motorways (compared with West Germany's 8,000 kilometres) there are 13,000 kilometres of trunk roads, which include some lengths of dual carriageway and some narrow, twisty sections. But even these roads still pass through some villages with streets just wide enough for a lorry to go through while traffic in the opposite direction has to wait.

In general, the further north one goes, the more adequate the roads are for the traffic which they carry. Wales and Scotland have been treated generously, with great lengths of nearly empty dual carriageways. Apart from the motorways which radiate from London, the roads in the south of England, which has the greatest load of traffic, must be among the most inadequate in Europe. In the south-west great lengths of single-track roads, including some to busy seaside resorts, still wind their way between high banks or hedges. In London very little has been done to improve the roads, and the average speed of travel in the central area is now about the same as a hundred years ago, when horses did the work. The motorway around London's outer edge was not completed until 1986, and parts of it have been clogged with crawling traffic for much of the time since then.

Around 1960 there were great schemes for new roads, including many city radial and inner-circle routes. A few have been carried out, but with every scheme the procedure for dealing with objections may take many years, with vast sums of money paid to barristers to argue before public inquiries. All new schemes can now be opposed on the ground that new urban roads simply increase the traffic, and its consequent pollution, until the overall position is no better than it was before. And it is pointed out that in central London, where the existing roads have been saturated for many years, the volume of road traffic has increased very little.

A quite different problem affects main inter-city roads. Vast sums of money are now being spent on maintaining major roads, to prevent them from collapsing under the weight of heavy lorry traffic; axle weights and volume have increased beyond earlier expectations. In twenty years more has been spent to stop the Severn Bridge from falling down than was spent in building it. But the revenue from the small tolls paid by lorries has covered only a small fraction of the expenditure which they have made necessary.

About 5,000 people have been killed in road accidents in each year since 1985 (reduced from 8,000 in 1965). The death rate per vehicle-kilometre is well below that in most other Western European countries (except Scandinavia); it has been consistently about half that in France. As the British roads are in general less adequate than the French, the difference seems to indicate that the British behave better on the roads, with more self-control and less aggressive attitudes. Even so, it is estimated that the money-cost of road accidents is equal to nearly 1 per cent of the gross national product.

4   Public Transport

British towns suffer from the same traffic congestion, noise and polluting fumes as all towns in the western world, but as yet only London, Newcastle, Glasgow and (to a small extent) Liverpool have useful railways going underground through the central areas. Elsewhere there are plans but they have little hope of making progress so long as public expenditure is restricted. In general the north has better public transport than the south, with cheap and frequent bus services using better roads with fewer cars to obstruct them.

Many British town buses have two decks, and the top deck is a good place from which to see the view. In the 1980s some competing services have been allowed, with varying success. In some places infrequent big buses have been replaced by more frequent smaller ones, which have led some travellers to go by bus instead of car. The more this happens, the less the congestion, the greater the scope for a better bus service.

In London the buses suffer from traffic congestion, and anyone who does not buy a special all-routes pass must pay separately for each bus ride, to the conductor if there is one, otherwise to the driver.

In the 1980s the difficulty of travel by road in London has increased the passengers on the underground railways. Although two new lines have been built through the central area in the past thirty years there is often extreme overcrowding. Stations have been refurbished at great cost, but the trains are unreliable in their operation, often stopping in the tunnels, between the stations.

The main train services, called 'inter-city', between London and the

A traffic jam in central London.

main towns to the north and west, were expected to cover their costs without subsidy by 1990. These trains run at least every hour, at standard fares. There is no need to reserve a seat, but there is some overcrowding. All the inter-city train routes have parallel inter-city buses which compete for passengers. However, the bus services between the inter-city railway stations and the surrounding small towns which have no railway any more, are slow, infrequent and not coordinated with trains.

The railways carry very little freight, and much of what they do carry consists of coal or oil moving from pitheads or ports to electric power stations. There is no subsidy for rail freight.

There are not many internal air services except between London and the big cities of the north and Scotland. Most international scheduled air services use London's main airport, Heathrow, which is served by an extension of the Piccadilly tube line. Heathrow's three old passenger terminals are grouped together, close to the tube station, but the new fourth terminal is far away, and served by a separate tube station.

London's second airport, Gatwick, is served by frequent main line trains of the British Rail system, on the Victoria to Brighton line. A third London airport at Stansted is now being expanded as air traffic grows beyond the capacity of Gatwick and Heathrow. All these three airports, together with the main Scottish ones, were nationalised, along with British Airways, in the 1940s, then sold to private shareholders in the 1980s. The plan to develop Stansted into a major airport goes back to 1961, but no work was done for twenty-five years. In the meantime many millions of pounds were spent on inquiries about airport policy, and the published reports issued in this time make a pile too big to carry. Better options were neglected or rejected, some of them for dubious reasons. The plan for a railway tunnel across the Channel, which would have given a little relief to London's airports, was abandoned in 1975 and then restarted, as an investment by the private sector, in 1987. It is due to be opened in 1993. A new connecting high-speed railway line on the English side, financed by the private sector, was proposed in 1988. Without it the tunnel's potential cannot be realised.

It remains to be seen whether the choices of the market will in the long run work better than the old attempts at comprehensive central planning.

Questions

TABLE 9.1

Types of dwelling in Great Britain (percentages)

	Overall	Top quarter: professional and managers	Bottom quarter: semi-skilled and unskilled
Detached house	19	40	7
Semi-detached house	33	30	30
Terraced house	29	18	36
Purpose-built flat	14	8	22
Converted flat	4	4	4
Owned outright	25	28	20
Owned with a mortgage	38	57	17
Rented from local authority, etc.	27	6	50
Rented privately	9	4	12
With job or business	2	4	2

1   Is the British preference for single houses unsuitable for a country with high population density?

TABLE 9.2

Average annual change in dwellling stock in the UK
(thousands)

	1961 -1970	1971 -1975	1976 -1980	1981	1982 -1986
New construction					
Public sector (in general, subsidised)	170	143	139	88	51
Private sector	198	178	146	118	152
Total new construction	368	320	284	106	203

2   Discuss the decrease in provision of public-sector housing.

How much do people travel, and by what means?

The Government regularly produces statistics about traffic. The total amount of travel within Great Britain, converted to averages, amounts to about 900 kilometres per person by car, 70 each by train and bus, and 8 to 10 each by pedal cycle, motor cycle and aeroplane. In the past 25 years the amount of travel by car and air has doubled, while travel by other means has not changed much.

3   What are the main advantages and disadvantages in the growth of travel by road?
4   What are the main arguments for and against the charging of tolls for the use of motorways?
5   Should governments give big subsidies to railways?

121

Patients waiting for treatment at a GP's surgery.

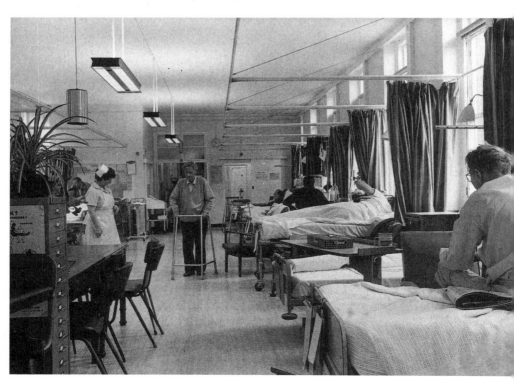

A ward in a National Health Service hospital.

The Welfare State

1 Social Security

It is now accepted in Britain that the state should ensure, as far as it can, that nobody should be without the necessities of life as the result of unemployment, old age, sickness or over-large families. The operations of the welfare state are in four main parts. First, there is the system of National Insurance. Everybody who is working is obliged to contribute a fixed amount each week to the National Insurance Fund, and this fund, which receives supplementary contributions from the proceeds of general taxation, is used for old age pensions and for paying out benefits for limited periods to people who are unemployed, or unable to earn because they are sick. Second, free or nearly free medical care is provided for everyone under the National Health Service, which is also financed partly by weekly contributions paid by people who are working, but mainly by payments by the state out of general taxation. Third, supplementary benefits are provided for people whose incomes are too low for them to be able to live at a minimum standard. Finally, there are services for the benefit of children, apart from the provision of education. These include allowances paid to parents in respect of each child, but subsidies for children's food have now been restricted to families who need them.

Every person who is working must make a single National Insurance contribution every week. The amount to be paid each week is a little more for employees than for people who are self-employed. In the case of employees, the responsibility for making the payments belongs to the employer, who must deduct part of each worker's wage or salary, and add larger sums himself. But the amount collected in contributions has regularly been little more than half of the total paid out in benefits based on contributions. Payments to retired people are much the biggest item. The deficit is paid for out of general taxation, along with the cost of the National Health Service. The insurance contributions tend to be regarded as though they were one source of revenue, similar to ordinary taxation.

The retirement pension, or 'old age pension' as it is popularly called, may be received by any man from the age of sixty-five (provided he has made his weekly contributions to the fund) if he ceases to work, and by any woman from the age of sixty. A man may continue to work full time after he is sixty-five, and in that case he gets no pension at first, but when he is over seventy he gets a bigger pension whether he works or not. The normal rate of pension is regularly increased with inflation, but is rather low in comparison with some other Western European countries.

There are in addition non-state methods of providing for retirement pensions. Some people have life insurance policies. Some contribute to their trade union pension funds, and then receive pensions from them when they retire. Most salaried or middle-class types of jobs have some system of 'superannuation', with the employer and employee making payments into a pension fund, and this system is spreading rapidly for manual workers too. Many people have one or more of these forms of old age insurance in addition to the state pension.

People who become unemployed, or unable to work because of sickness, receive payments from the National Insurance Fund at the same rate as retirement pensioners. The amount of time for which a person is entitled to receive these benefits (up to about twelve months) depends, to some extent, on contributions into the insurance fund. Sickness benefit is paid for up to twenty-eight weeks, at the same rate as a retirement pension; after twenty-eight weeks it is replaced by invalidity benefit, at a lower rate, together with supplements if necessary. However, a person in a middle-class salaried job may well be paid a full salary for long periods of absence through sickness. The detailed provisions for state benefits to people who have long illnesses affect mainly manual workers. Employers tend to treat their salaried employees more favourably than their weekly-paid manual workers; the welfare state goes a little of the way towards redressing this difference.

The system of payments to people on the basis of proved need has been altered many times. It is operated through local offices of the Department of Social Security, not by local government councils. The principle is that everyone should be able to live at a minimum standard; these payments do not depend on insurance contributions. People may get regular weekly payments, help with rent and various extra payments too if they show that without such help their incomes would be below a certain minimum. In very cold weather old people may get extra payments to cover their extra costs for heating; these payments were increased in 1987 after reports of old people suffering from hypothermia. On the other hand the 1980s have brought new restrictions to prevent abuse, and young people who have left school may be required to undergo training if they do not get paid work. People who suffer from disablement or handicap get special payments according to their circumstances – though not always enough to provide them with the most expensive devices to help them.

A weekly allowance is paid in respect of every child, whatever the parents' income may be. There are also special allowances for single parents, payable on proof of need. But in 1987 and 1988 the general children's allowance was not increased to keep up with inflation, so its real value declined. There were signs that the Government was considering the possibility of ending the unconditional allowances for children, on the ground that money handed out to rich parents would be better spent on increased payments to the poor. Several benefits for children were ended long ago, such as free milk and orange juice. In the 1980s they had to pay more for lunch at school, and for school buses, unless their parents had very low incomes.

2   The National Health Service

The National Health Service came into existence in 1948, to give completely free medical treatment of every kind to everyone needing it. Since then some payment has been brought in for one item after another, beginning in 1951 when patients had to pay a small fixed amount for pills or medicine prescribed for them. Children, pregnant women, old people and the poor have been exempted from some of these charges, but in 1988 the Government began to abolish some general exemptions for pensioners.

People who are ill go first to see their general practitioners (GPs), who treat minor illnesses themselves. These family doctors work alone or in partnerships from surgeries or bigger urban medical centres, and when necessary go to see patients in their homes. Everyone is normally on the list of a general practitioner (or family doctor), who keeps full records of all treatments and over the years gets to know the 2,000 or more people on his or her list. Each GP is paid a fixed amount related to the number of patients on the list.

General practitioners refer people to hospital, if necessary, for more specialised treatment, also free of charge both at outpatients' clinics and for those who have to stay in hospital.

Doctors and others who work in hospitals are paid salaries, full time or part time, graded according to their jobs, with consultants at the top.

England is divided into fourteen regions based on university medical schools (not on counties); each region is divided into about ten to fifteen districts, based on major hospitals. Regions and districts have governing boards appointed by the Secretary of State for Health.

Most dental treatment is carried out in the dentists' surgeries which are scattered around all towns, though difficult cases are sent to dental hospitals. The dentists are paid from health service funds for each item of treatment. At first their patients did not have to pay, but later part-payment became necessary, and now people must pay even for check-ups which find nothing wrong. Only children and a few others are exempt.

Eye tests are usually done in opticians' shops; they too must be paid for, as well as any glasses which are needed. Payment for the eye tests was introduced in 1988, although it was argued that some people would be deterred from going for tests which could have detected incipient blindness in good time. People who are found to need further treatment to their eyes are sent to eye hospitals, where treatment is free.

People do not go directly to hospital unless they are victims of accidents or for some other reason need urgent treatment. They go to the casualty departments, which, unlike GPs' surgeries, work continuously, mostly receiving people brought in by Health Service ambulances.

Public opinion has always been extremely favourable to the health service, with majorities in opinion polls expressing general satisfaction with it and a strong wish that it should continue. Statistics suggest that it has given people reasonably effective service. Expectation of life has risen, although at a slower rate than in many comparable Western European countries. However, one purpose of the Labour government which created the service in 1948 was to ensure that people's access to medical care of all kinds should not depend on ability to pay. This purpose was egalitarian. At that time people in the highest socio-economic categories suffered less serious illness and lived longer than people in the lowest categories. These differences have continued with very little change, although the proportion of people living in unhealthy houses because of poverty has declined.

Various complex explanations can be suggested for the continuance of class differentials in health and life expectancy. These include differences in life-styles, including diet, for which individuals are personally responsible. But it can be said that, in so far as the National Health Service had originally an egalitarian purpose, some aspects of this purpose have not been achieved.

When the National Health Service was established many doctors argued that, if doctors were not paid for each item of treatment given, they

TABLE 10.2

National Health Service personnel
(thousands)

	1970	1981	1986
Medical and dental	44	50	52
Nursing	430	493	506
Other	454	485	449
Family practioner services			
Doctors (GPs)	24	27	31
Other	24	27	19

1 Do the figures indicate a deterioration in the National Health Service?

2 Although many people aged over sixty-five depend entirely on state pensions, a growing proportion have substantial other incomes, including non-state pensions. Would it be right to make the rate of state pension depend on the means of the individual?

3 Should state children's allowances be means-tested?

4 For the 1990s Mrs Thatcher's government has proposed changes to the National Health Service which would involve competition between doctors and hospitals, and force them to be more careful to restrain their expenditure. What do you think about this?

5 Do you favour the idea that jobs like cleaning and providing food for hospitals should be done by firms under contract, rather than by the hospitals' own staffs?

Primary school children in an art class.

Secondary school students working on a woodwork project.

11

Schools and Universities

1 The Educational System

Even more than in other countries, discussion of education in Britain tends to be dominated by argument about its effects on inequality and privilege in society. This is partly because the state was slow in building up its role in education. The private sector (as it is now called) filled the vacuum for such a long time that it is still significant.

Free and compulsory education, funded by the state and guaranteed by law, became available in 1870 for children aged from five to ten. Some primary schools had already been provided by churches and charities, and in time these bodies agreed to having their schools taken over by the new system, which was run by local authorities (education committees of county councils) most of whose costs were covered by grants from the central government.

Meanwhile, secondary education was left to the private sector, though the main day schools in towns received grants directly from the central government. The grants covered a large part of their costs, and up to half of their pupils, chosen for merit, paid no fees. This direct grant system was ended in 1976, when a few of these schools joined the state system, while the majority became wholly self-supporting. Meanwhile, the most prestigious secondary boarding schools have always remained wholly independent of the state system.

Before 1944 the state system developed in two ways. The school leaving age had been raised by stages to fourteen, and some local education authorities had developed their own grammar schools. In 1944 a new law raised the leaving age to fifteen. All education beyond the age of eleven became 'secondary'. At that age most children went to secondary modern schools, while about a fifth of all children, chosen by examination, went to grammar schools, aiming to gain certificates at sixteen, and then eighteen, leading to further education

By the 1960s, this division of children in the state system was criticised for sustaining inequalities. The school leaving age was raised to sixteen, and by 1980 almost all state secondary schools were 'comprehensive', taking all children from their areas at the age of eleven. This change, combined with the abolition of direct grants to some private sector schools, has tended to widen the gap between the private and state sectors of secondary education, and to increase some inequalities which had previously been reduced.

In 1986 a new GCSE qualification, (General Certificate of Secondary Education), was introduced. This was designed to give scope for children of all types and inclinations to pass, at about the age of sixteen, in at least some subjects corresponding with their talents. The certificates are awarded on the basis, partly of examinations, partly of course work, partly of work on projects undertaken by the children. The tests are administered by several different examining boards which are independent of central and local government.

Children who continue their education after sixteen, in what is commonly called the 'sixth form', prepare themselves to try to gain vocational or professional certificates or diplomas. Those who hope to continue after eighteen, at universities or other higher-level colleges, aim to gain advanced-level GCSE certificates, usually in three subjects, and entry to the universities, etc. is based on the grades (A, B, C, D, E) gained.

There is no formal division of the teaching profession between primary and secondary school teachers, though primary teachers are normally trained in three-year Bachelor of Education courses, enabling them to teach young children in all subjects, while secondary teachers are prepared in one-year postgraduate pedagogical courses after getting university degrees in the subjects which they will eventually teach. There is a single pay scale, with additions to the salaries of teachers with special responsibilities. It is rare, and becoming rarer, for teachers to move, during their careers, between state and private-sector schools.

There are some Roman Catholic secondary schools in the state system, and recently some Muslim ones have been added. As with the Church of England primary schools, the religious bodies provide only a very small part of the capital costs, and in return determine the content of religious teaching, and influence the appointment of heads and some other teachers. To this extent Britain has dealt with the problem of religious education quite satisfactorily. In the ordinary state schools the law requires that Christian instruction be given, but this has developed mainly into informal study of different religions. However, in 1988 the Government proposed that all children should participate in religious worship, either in assemblies or in classrooms (with individual parents having the right to withdraw their children from these occasions). The proposal caused so much consternation among teachers that it is unlikely that it will be effective.

The academic year begins in September, after the summer holidays, and is divided into three 'terms', with the intervals between them formed by the Christmas and Easter holidays. The exact dates of the holidays vary from area to area, being in general about two weeks at Christmas and Easter, plus a week in the middle of each term, and five weeks in the summer.

Day schools mostly work Mondays to Fridays only, from about 9 a.m. to between 3 and 4 p.m. Lunch is provided and parents pay most of the cost unless their income is low enough to entitle them to free children's meals. Subsidies for school meals were reduced in the 1980s, and many children who cannot go home for lunch now bring their own sandwiches.

2   State Education

In the past the central government has not involved itself directly in matters of the school curriculum, though it appoints about 500 experienced teachers as Her Majesty's Inspectors (HMI). Each school is visited quite frequently by an Inspector and every few years a team of HMIs carries out a thorough examination of each school's work. Their reports include criticism and advice, relating to general and particular matters, and to the work and methods of individual teachers. They have great influence, but no defined powers, though it seems likely that their role will be enhanced in the 1990s by the effects of a new law of 1988.

In Scotland, Wales and Northern Ireland the schools and colleges are run by local education authorities under the general responsibility of the Secretaries of State for these three countries, and of their central education offices in Edinburgh, Cardiff and Belfast. But these three are members of the UK cabinet, and their policies in principle form parts of the policy of the UK government (see Chapter 13 pp.178–81). In England the Secretary of State for Education and Science has overall responsibility.

Primary schools

In primary schools the first two years, beginning at the age of five, are spent on informal development of expression and ability to concentrate. Often children stay with the same teacher all the time for this whole 'infant' period. More formal 'junior level' teaching begins at the age of seven, though at this stage there is more concern with making children interested than with traditional instruction. Competitiveness in the learning process is not encouraged, though there is now a reaction against extreme permissiveness, and in favour of increased attention to the teaching of basic skills and knowledge.

Secondary schools

Although almost all state secondary schools are now comprehensive schools, the equalising purpose of the system has not altogether been achieved. All comprehensive secondary schools may be intended to be of equal standard, but in some schools far bigger proportions of the pupils perform well in the certificate examinations than in others. The highest success rates tend to be in schools in comfortable suburban areas, the lowest in those parts of big towns where the social indicators are least favourable.

Parents may ask for their children to go to one school rather than another: a school with a good reputation may attract the more academically inclined. Even in the most favoured schools there are problems with a proportion of the pupils, but the majority of comprehensive schools provide a thorough academic education. In a minority of schools, mainly in inner cities, the teachers' main task is to keep disruption to a minimum. In spite of the efforts of school attendance officers many pupils attend irregularly, and have little interest in their work when they do attend.

The old practice of 'streaming', or teaching children in classes separated according to ability, has been unfashionable but is still used. Mixed-ability classes are obviously less 'elitist' than streamed ones, and some inconclusive evidence suggests that children of high ability do not develop more quickly when they are separated from the rest. This argument is not settled; it has political implications.

Outside the academic curriculum there is great concern with the development of the child's personality. Clubs are encouraged for the joint pursuit of interests in nature, such as bird-watching, or music, dancing or drama. There is also usually a pastoral system, through which each teacher meets an assigned group of twenty or thirty pupils regularly to discuss problems of the world in general, and gives advice on choice of courses and, if necessary, on personal problems.

The approach to education has changed in the past thirty years. It is now widely accepted that it is not enough for children simply to absorb and remember information. They should be equipped to evaluate and criticise the information they receive, and to find out things for themselves. The content of education should as far as practicable be relevant to real life. Language teaching should make use of typical situations of tourists or business people. The rules of grammar and syntax are not emphasised at the early stages. Children learn about the essential relations between figures rather than mathematical procedures – and they should grow up with computing skills. They are encouraged to undertake projects on their own account, often in pairs or in groups.

In the 1980s it was not clear whether the new methods were having a positive effect. The proportion of pupils gaining ordinary and advanced certificates at sixteen and eighteen had increased a little, but too many children were leaving school with very low standards of literacy and numeracy. Britain was not doing well in international comparisons of educational attainment.

In 1988 a new law on education was passed. The role of the local education authorities was to be reduced, while that of the central government was to be increased, along with the autonomy of individual school heads and governing bodies. For the first time a basic national curriculum was established, with targets of proficiency in the 'core' subjects of science, mathematics and English, with in general at least one foreign language (usually French). Certain minimum standards should be set, appropriate to successive age levels (probably seven, eleven and fourteen).

In 1987–88 a committee of acknowledged experts, whose chairman was a mathematician and university vice-chancellor, was appointed to suggest objectives in the teaching of English. Its report implied that the movement away from traditional aspects such as grammar and syntax had gone too far; children aged eleven ought to know about the structure of language and about things such as verbs and nouns.

Every school has a 'senior management team' (SMT), and every teacher must under contract do 1,265 hours of 'SMT-directed time' in a year – most of it in class with pupils, the rest attending meetings or on other specified activities. A typical forty-year-old secondary-school teacher has also to spend undirected time preparing for classes at several different levels, including one or two for academic seventeen-year-olds, marking written work and writing reports on pupils. The total of work hours in the year is likely to be more than the 1,750 hour average of non-manual workers. But the relative pay of teachers with management responsibilities has been increased, to give more incentive for a competitive attitude within the profession.

Another innovation is an increase in the detailed responsibility of each school's Senior Management Team for the school's budget. The amount is to be related to the number of pupils, and parents are to have more choice between schools, so that a school which attracts more pupils will get more money to spend. Also, the role of the school governing body is to be increased, along with that of the parents' representatives. It is hoped that, with an element of competition between schools in the state sector, standards will be improved and that money will be used more effectively.

One difficulty is similar to that which affects many other public services. Modern technology demands more expenditure on computers and other types of school equipment, to which high priority is given. There are innumerable reasons why attempts to improve standards demand more money. But the current Government's first priorities are concerned with economy: to curb inflation, to reduce taxes, and hence to restrain public expenditure. Some teachers have been buying chalk, drawing pins and so on in the shops because they have no time in the school day to get them from the stores. Some buy paint and decorate dingy classrooms in the holidays, even in quite modern buildings, because the authorities have no funds for these essential purposes. When teachers compare their working conditions, pay and status in society with those of their friends who have become accountants, they can easily feel aggrieved and resentful. There is a serious lack of teachers of mathematics, science and crafts, because teachers with qualifications in these subjects are leaving the profession and are not being replaced by new ones.

The Government's general lack of enthusiasm for activities in the public sector has produced hostile reactions in the teaching profession. All through the 1980s the main teachers' union engaged in periodic 'industrial action', protesting against pay and working conditions by sporadic disruption of school activities.

The number of children of secondary-school age fell by nearly 20 per cent in the 1980s, because of the changes in the birthrate, and by more than this in the inner cities. The numbers overall will increase a little in the 1990s. The Government intends that more parental choice will ensure that resources will go to the most efficient schools. The innovations are not altogether encouraging to those whose dedication is to the teaching of children to the best of their ability, rather than to the pursuit of competitive careers. It seems that a large proportion of teachers dislike the new directions, and it is not clear how permanent they will be, or what their effect will be.

Students at Eton, one of Britain's most famous public schools.

3   Independent Schools

Private-sector education is based originally on boys' schools founded by public-spirited men of substance in the sixteenth and seventeenth centuries. They were called 'public schools' to distinguish them from small private schools run by individuals. Many others were added later, together with a whole range of girls' schools, mainly around 1840 and after. The term 'public school' has now become obviously absurd and its meaning is uncertain. For statistical purposes it applies to all the schools which are members of the Headmasters' Conference (HMC), of which there are about 250, all with strong sixth forms for pupils aged between sixteen and eighteen. But it is often used more broadly, or more narrowly to refer to the boarding (residential) schools in the HMC.

Until about 1970 nearly all the private-sector schools were for boys or girls only. However, since then some of the former boys' schools have

139

begun to take in girls as well, some only at sixth-form level, some at all ages, and more than half now take girls. Meanwhile, the girls' schools continue without boys, but are losing many of their best potential pupils to the former boys-only schools. There is a girls' schools association which is equivalent to the HMC, but in 1989 almost a tenth of the girls-only schools had headmasters, while not one of the former boys' (now coeducational) schools belonging to the HMC had a headmistress.

Most schools give scholarships for special merit to some of their pupils, with a reduction of fees depending partly on the parents' means. More than a tenth of all pupils in these schools as a whole have scholarships of this kind, and a somewhat smaller number now have help with their fees from the Government's assisted-places scheme.

The private sector has two parts which are more or less distinct, though the borderline is not clear. Some schools, mostly in towns, are wholly or mainly for day pupils. Most of these are for children aged 11–18, like the state secondary schools. Most of their pupils come to them aged eleven from state primary schools, on the basis of selective and competitive examinations, though some schools have their own primary sections attached to them, from which eleven-year-olds may move up if they are academically good enough. Most of these schools received direct grants from the government for some decades before 1976, but have now become wholly independent.

The independent day schools in big towns have much in common with the old principal lycées and Gymnasiums or equivalent in Western Europe, though that resemblance has been reduced by the ending of the direct-grant system in 1976. Some of them, such as Manchester Grammar School (founded in 1515) and Bristol Grammar School (1532), and several of those in London, have great reputations for academic excellence, and are seen as much-respected civic institutions.

The major boarding schools, or 'public schools' in the narrow sense, are peculiar to Britain, and especially to the southern half of England, where most of them are situated. More than any other part of the educational system, they distinguish Britain from other countries. About 100 are mainly residential ('boarding') schools, though many of these take day pupils too. These are mainly for children aged 13–18, and receive thirteen year olds on the basis of entrance examinations, partly from their own attached junior schools, partly from quite small private 'preparatory' ('prep') schools for children aged 7–13, partly from state schools.

Although few parents send their children to them for religious reasons, these schools have their own substantial chapels, where their chaplains or headmasters conduct services according to the prescriptions of the foundation. Some are Catholic, but most are Church of England. Around 1900 many headmasters were clergymen, and some of them went on to become bishops; but this is so no more. The chapels, with their choirs, have always provided a stimulus for development of musical appreciation.

Over the past 100 years the inner group of about 100 mainly boarding schools has had a profound effect on English social attitudes. By their nature and existence they have emphasised a sense of class division. Although less then 2 per cent of all men have been educated in such schools, these include most high court judges, directors of banks and insurance companies and Conservative MPs. Contacts made at school may open the way to good jobs – though less so now than in the past. One of these schools, Eton, is perhaps better known by name outside its own country than any other school in the world. It was founded by King Henry VI in 1440, across the Thames from Windsor Castle. More than half of all peers who have inherited their titles are old Etonians, and in 1963 Sir Alec Douglas-Home was not only the third Etonian prime minister in succession but also the eighteenth out of the thirty-six in 200 years. Yet only one man out of 1,500 was a pupil there. It is like the other public schools in many ways, but has its special customs. Boys still dress every day for class in morning suits, as though for a wedding.

Most boarding public schools are in small towns or villages within about 250 kilometres of London, and have about 700 pupils. They flourished and expanded during the last century of the British Empire. They have been much concerned to develop in their pupils a strong sense of duty, obedience combined with ability to exercise authority, and a habit of suppressing private feelings. Loyalty to a group has been encouraged by the system under which a school of 700 boys would be divided into about ten 'houses', with selected older boys as prefects (or monitors, or praeposters: each school has its private language). Until quite recently the prefects imposed a strict discipline, often with brutal punishments. Good cricket and rugby football players won great prestige.

The prefects still survive, but the old brutality does not. The houses have fewer silly rules, and give pupils more scope to follow their own interests and more privacy. The schools have shown skill in adapting themselves to new values, with more attention to music and the arts as well as academic work as distinct from team games. Many of their teachers, who are mostly male and called 'masters', stay at the same school all through their working lives, and do not count their hours of work.

The normal fees for two children would be more than a senior teacher's total earnings. Yet the schools are full, with pupils' fees paid partly by grandparents, or from savings or long-term insurance policies. Inevitably, they are reserved mainly for the well-to-do, including many pupils sent to them from overseas. Objectively, these schools probably have more merit now than fifty years ago, but they are still the object of some egalitarian resentment. The schools have small classes and high standards. Egalitarians do not like them, and at one time hoped that they would lose pupils until one by one they would join the state system or collapse. Indeed, some of their pupils and former pupils feel embarrassed by their privileged education. But in the 1980s most independent schools of all types have had more applicants for admission than before. They have been helped by the poor reputation of the state comprehensive schools, and by the huge growth in the incomes of the highly-paid people, along with the huge cuts in the top rates of income tax.

4   Education after School

Most formal education after school is done in the various technical and other colleges, of which there is at least one in every town. There are more than 500, big and small, specialised or more general, mostly maintained by their local education authorities. Some of their students do full-time courses, but many have jobs and attend classes in the evenings, or on one or two days a week, preparing themselves for diplomas or certificates of proficiency in the innumerable skills which a modern society needs. These courses may be suitable for people who have left school at sixteen, or at a higher level. Some colleges prepare students for certificates of education, supplementing the work of equivalent level done in ordinary schools. The variety of colleges and courses is so great that it is impossible to make general statements about them. The students are of all ages, including older people developing new skills. In general the bigger the college the greater the range of its courses, though attempts are made within each local area to provide courses suitable for most of the people who want to obtain qualifications for their careers.

In general, people who undertake 'further education' beyond the age of eighteen pay fees for their tuition as well as their living costs, though for a long time until around 1980 the tuition fees were very low, and almost all the costs were covered by grants from public funds – that is, the proceeds of taxation.

However, students living in Britain may receive grants from the local authorities of the counties where they have their homes. The amount of the grant depends on their parents' income. The maximum, payable to people with low incomes, is fixed by the central government, and is supposed to be enough to cover the whole of the student's costs. However, students have always argued that the grants are not enough. Wealthy parents have to pay almost all the costs.

In the 1980s the government has tried to reduce the proportion of the cost of further education paid out of the proceeds of taxation. Already before 1980 the tuition fees for students coming from outside Britain were increased. Later, any grants from tax-funds were set at such a level that all tuition fees had to be increased.

For higher-level studies the main qualification is the 'first' degree of Bachelor (of Arts, Science, etc.) which can be attained by students who pass their university examinations, or in some cases other examinations of equivalent level. This normally involves at least three years of full-time study after passing the advanced level certificate of education at the age of about eighteen, so most people who become BA, BSc, etc. do so at the age of at least twenty-one. First degrees in medicine require six years of study, some others four. It is now quite usual for students in subjects such as engineering to spend periods during their degree courses away from their academic studies, in industrial locations, so that they may get practical experience. A student of a foreign language normally spends a year in a country where that language is spoken. Bachelors' degrees are usually awarded on the basis of answers to several three-hour examinations together with practical work or long essays or dissertations written in conjunction with class work. Degrees are classified. About a tenth (or less) of candidates win first-class honours degrees, three-quarters second-class (divided nearly equally into two groups), the rest third-class, or pass without honours, or fail.

Some students continue to study for degrees of Master (of Arts, Science, etc.) which often need two further years of study, with examination papers and substantial dissertations. A minority go on further, preparing theses which must make original contributions to knowledge, for the degree of Doctor of Philosophy (PhD). Higher-degree study is more common among students of natural or applied sciences than among those studying the arts – that is, philosophy, history, English or foreign languages – or the social sciences such as economics, sociology, political science or law. But many people who gain first degrees in these subjects often go on to more practical training courses which lead to various kinds of professional qualifications.

England is unusual among European countries in having had only two universities until 1820 – though there were already four in Scotland in the sixteenth century, when Scotland was still a separate kingdom. England's two ancient universities, Oxford and Cambridge, were the only ones in the country for almost 500 years from 1348. They still have a special preeminence, as well as many characteristics peculiar to themselves, and are best considered separately.

The beginning of the modern university system came with the grant of a charter to the University of London in 1836. It consisted then of two recently-founded colleges, and others were added at various later dates. Another university, at Durham in the north, was founded in 1832, but it remained small until quite recently. The University of Wales was established in 1893, with one constituent college in each of two big towns and two small ones.

During the nineteenth century colleges which were founded in the biggest English towns began to prepare students for external degrees of the University of London. At various dates between 1900 and 1962 these university colleges were granted charters as full universities, with the right to confer degrees on their own account. During the 1960s they all expanded fast, and seven completely new universities were founded in addition, all of them establishing campuses on the edges of historic towns without much industry. Meanwhile, some of the local authorities' technical colleges had developed their courses to a higher level, and eight of these were given their own charters in 1966–67. So within three years the number of universities in England doubled, to 32; and in Scotland too four new ones were added.

Even this expansion was not enough to cope with the rise in the demand for university-level study, and the growth of university-level courses in the local technical colleges. In 1964 a new body was set up, the Council for National Academic Awards (CNAA). Any college which has developed a course at university level may apply to it, asking to have the course recognised as a degree-level course in its own right. In that case the CNAA looks thoroughly at the structure and content of the courses, the teaching facilities of every kind and the proposed system of examination. If the CNAA is satisfied, the college may then organise its own syllabuses, teaching and examinations, and successful students are then awarded CNAA degrees.

Soon after 1964 various courses were recognised for CNAA degrees, and within a few years thirty colleges were raised to the newly-invented category of 'polytechnics'. All of these, still run by local councils, were fully established by 1973. In addition to the polytechnics, more than 100 other colleges now also provide some courses leading to CNAA degrees of university standard. In 1988 the Education Reform Act provided for a change in the status of these colleges. Twenty-eight of them, as well as all the polytechnics, became independent institutions, with a status akin to

Cambridge University students at the entrance to their college.

The University of Sussex, a modern campus university.

that of universities, getting some of their funds from fees, grants from government-funded research councils, public and private-sector organisations, endowments (if any) and donations. But the main source of funds is the state itself, giving money for capital and current costs to each institution. In future these normal government grants will come through the Universities Funding Council or the Polytechnic and Colleges Funding Council, as the case may be, and these bodies will assess the quality of the institutions before deciding how to distribute grants among them.

As distinct from the colleges and polytechnics, the universities have always been independent of both local authorities and the state. Each has a council as its effective governing body (composed of professors, lecturers' and students' representatives and local notables) and a vice-chancellor (appointed by the council) as an academic chief. Each university has its own organisation, but usually there are about six faculties, each containing a group of departments (for example a faculty of Arts for history, English, philosophy and languages).

Lecturers are appointed on the basis of their achievements in their first-degree examinations and postgraduate research. Their security of tenure in their jobs is being reduced. A lecturer who produces published research papers which are praised by the academic community may be promoted to the grade of reader. To be appointed to a professor's chair it is usually necessary to move to another university. Success in obtaining grants of money for research projects helps towards promotion.

Apart from lecture courses the teaching is done mostly in laboratories or in tutorial groups for three or four students, or seminars for about ten. Students are required to write numerous essays or seminar papers, which may be discussed in the group meetings. Some of these may be used for assessment towards the class of degree awarded. There are usually not more than twelve students for each teacher in a department, and there is plenty of personal contact between them.

Each university's faculties issue prospectuses describing their courses. Anyone wanting to enter a university gets copies of several of these and an application form from the Universities' Central Council for Admissions, on which to enter applications for up to five courses in different universities. Applicants then go to visit the universities to which they have applied, and may be interviewed by lecturers, who eventually decide which of the applicants to accept, mainly on the basis of the grades obtained in the advanced-level certificate examinations. Each course has a quota of new students which ought not to be exceeded, so entry to each course is in effect competitive. Perhaps as a result of this restricted entry, only about an eighth of students who start university courses fail to complete them.

The great majority of students are in universities far from their homes; Bristol University has very few students who live near it, but many people who live in Bristol are at other universities. Each university has halls of residence with enough room for all or most of the first-year students, and in most cases for others too. For their last years of study most live in rented flats.

The preference for studying at universities away from home is probably linked with the old importance of the boarding public schools, and with the old preeminence of Oxford and Cambridge, which were for so long the only universities. As recently as 1950 these two together had almost as many students as all the other English universities outside London. Now they have less than a tenth of all university students, but they have had a big influence on the development of the university system, including the use of small groups for teaching. Their preeminence is diminishing, but not extinct.

These two ancient universities have, through the centuries, had a major role in English politics – Oxford more than Cambridge. Of the nine prime ministers since 1955 Mrs Thatcher was the seventh to have been to Oxford University. In 1988 her cabinet of twenty-one included seven who had been to Oxford, seven to Cambridge; two had been to old Scottish universities, one to London, none to any other university in England. The top civil servants have a similar background. This preponderance of Oxford and Cambridge graduates among the political élite (and among MPs in general) has declined, but it is still significant.

With about 10,000 first-degree students each, and over 2,000 post-graduates, Oxford and Cambridge are not big by modern standards. In most respects they are similar to each other, so a general description of one could apply to the other as well.

Apart from newly-developed small colleges for postgraduates, Oxford has more than twenty separate colleges, all rather like small independent universities. Sixteen of them already existed in 1600, when a few were already well over 200 years old, scattered among the streets of what is now the middle part of this town of about 100,000 people. Each college has within its precincts a hall, chapel, common rooms, library, lecture rooms, old and new buildings where half or two-thirds of the students and some staff live. Each college has between 200 and 400 undergraduate students and around thirty or more fellows (colloquially, 'dons'), who teach small groups as well as forming the college governing body. Nearly all the fellows (called by some other title in a few colleges) also hold office as university lecturers or professors, and are paid partly by the university, partly by their colleges. For each subject there is a university organisation resembling the departments in the other universities. Each college has a chief, who may be entitled Master, Warden, Provost, Rector, Principal, President or Dean.

For lecture courses, which are centrally organised, students go to other colleges or to the central lecture rooms, which are also used for the university's examinations. Teaching and research in sciences must be mainly in university laboratories.

All the colleges now take both men and women students, except for two of the five which were founded for women about 100 years ago. This change has been a major revolution of the past twenty years; so too has been the modernisation of the students' rooms on the old college staircases, with proper plumbing, baths and central heating systems.

With their old college buildings Oxford and Cambridge are inevitably visited by countless tourists, who are allowed to go within some college precincts, including the best gardens, at least on summer afternoons. The fifteenth-century chapel of King's College, Cambridge is one of England's finest churches, and the chapel of Oxford's grandest college (called Christ Church – or more familiarly and with a curious arrogance, 'The House') serves as the cathedral of the diocese. Oxford's 400-year old Bodleian Library, like that of Cambridge, is entitled, by long-established law, to receive free of charge a copy of every book published in the United Kingdom.

Some of the colleges in both universities are very wealthy, owning vast areas of land all over England. But much of the revenue from all this property is absorbed by the additional costs which arise from the maintenance of ancient buildings and providing everything that is needed for any university at an exceptionally high quality. For their basic expenditure Oxford and Cambridge, like other universities, became accustomed to dependence on the grants which the central government distributed in the period of expansion in roughly 1950–75. Since 1975 they, like other universities, have had to adapt themselves to steadily less generous government financing.

After 1970 the universities, old and new, continued to expand, encouraged by increasing government grants. But then the climate changed. The grants stopped growing. Suddenly the universities had to abandon their long-term plans, and soon they faced the need to cut their costs. They were forced to increase their fees for students from overseas, then for British residents as well – though those from families with low incomes still have their fees and living costs covered by local grants. Staff were encouraged to retire before the normal age, and many of those who did retire could not be replaced. The drive for economy continued in the 1980s. The universities were encouraged to try to supplement their funds from non-government sources, particularly for research projects. They have tried hard, with some success, to fill their buildings with conferences in vacations.

One new venture was the founding of a new independent university at Buckingham, 40 kilometres from Oxford. It is financed entirely by students' fees and private contributions, and by 1983 it was solidly established. It then received a charter enabling it to grant its own degrees. By 1988 there were 700 students. They can cover the work of a normal three-year course in two years by having no long summer vacation.

Meanwhile there has been great progress with adult education. For a long time university extra-mural departments have provided a great range of evening classes, in courses of varying length, often as joint ventures with the Workers' Educational Association. Some of these classes are led by full-time extra-mural tutors, others by regular lecturers in their spare time. A recent change of policy has enabled some of these courses to end with formal examinations, and diplomas for the successful students.

On a bigger scale is the Open University, which developed quickly in the 1970s. It was devised to satisfy the needs of working people of any age who wish to study in their spare time for degrees. It has a centre at the new town of Milton Keynes, between Oxford and Cambridge. Its full-time staff have produced a whole library of short coursebooks which anyone can buy by post or from any major bookshop. They devise courses which they present on one of the BBC's television channels and by radio. Most course work is run by part-time tutors (many of whom are lecturers at other universities); these are scattered around the country, and meet students to discuss their work at regular intervals. There are short residential summer courses. The students are of all ages, some of them retired. They may spread their studies over several years, and choose their courses to suit their individual needs and preferences. Over 100,000 people are enrolled, in all parts of the country.

The Open University has helped greatly towards the ideal of education accessible to everyone who aspires to it, at every level. For those retired people who do not want to work for diplomas or degrees there is a University of the Third Age, with about 100 centres. It has almost no formal structure except a system of communication which helps small groups to form themselves spontaneously to study. It gets no government funds, and collects small subscriptions from its participants.

Fashions in education change. The great rise of sociology in the 1960s soon collapsed, to be replaced by an even greater burgeoning of business studies and of training in the skills of management. Modern government policies cannot afford to neglect the role of education in developing the skills needed in the contemporary world – not only in applied sciences, but in the numeracy, at different levels, required in a world where computers have an increasing role, and also, in a quite different direction, in the ability to make effective use of languages other than English. There is no doubt that more Dutch and Scandinavian people can perform better in English than the British can in any other language. The Japanese may be less competent with foreign languages even than the British, but their mathematical skills, as well as others, have been shown to be superior.

It is partly for this reason that Mrs Thatcher's government was rather more supportive in its attitude to the polytechnics than to the older universities. Most polytechnic students study applied sciences, management or business studies. Their provision for languages is in general directed to the development of practical competence, including ability to cope with the special forms of language needed for aspects of the contemporary world's activities. It is less easy to measure the immediate practical utility of studying Racine and Molière, or even Anouilh and Sartre. There is, in general, a new emphasis on the role of education in preparing people for their future functions in the economy.

Questions

TABLE 11.1

Number of pupils per teacher			
	1971	1981	1987
Public-sector schools			
Primary	27.1	22.3	21.8
Secondary	17.8	16.4	15.4
Private-sector schools	13.0	13.1	11.6

1   In a MORI opinion poll in 1987 almost half the respondents said that they would send their children to private-sector schools if they could afford to. Is the role of the private sector a positive or a negative influence on education as a whole?

a cathedral. The cathedrals and hundreds of smaller churches, built between the eleventh century and King Henry VIII's time, are modern England's greatest glory, used by the Church of England; they help to identify it with the continuity of the nation. But the state does not make itself responsible for the physical upkeep of the buildings, which has to be paid for by voluntary contributions. For tourists there are shops and restaurants within the precincts of many cathedrals.

Similarly, the clergy are not paid by the state, but out of the Church's own funds, supplemented by money from parishioners. Most of the vicars in the parishes now live in ordinary small houses; the grand vicarages built 100 or 200 years ago are too big for them. They are in general paid less than the average industrial wage.

England is divided into forty-two dioceses, each with a bishop. Every diocese has a cathedral as its central church, though the bishop is concerned with the diocese and its parishes and not with the cathedral in particular. Each of the great old cathedrals has a dean and five or six residentiary canons (collectively called dean and chapter) who are together responsible for the cathedral and its services. There is often also a choir school, whose boys, together with the lay clerks, or men of the choir, provide fine music at matins and evensong each day. The canons live in elegant houses round the cathedral 'close'; some of them may also hold office as archdeacons, with administrative responsibilities in the diocese. Bishops are appointed by the Queen, who acts, in this as in all other matters, on the Prime Minister's advice. Long ago, prime ministers used this power 'politically' but now they have little reason for doing so. In 1975 a new system was introduced whereby the Prime Minister is advised by a committee, with representatives of the diocese and of the central body of the Church. As he or she has the constitutional responsibility for what he or she tells the Queen, he or she is not obliged to take notice of the Church's wishes, but it can safely be assumed that he or she does so.

The two Archbishops, of Canterbury and York, and twenty-four senior bishops have seats in the House of Lords, but rarely go there. When the Lords debate a moral or social issue at least one bishop normally speaks, expressing a Christian rather than a party point of view. The bishops have been on the 'liberal' side on issues such as birth control and abortion, and have vigorously opposed all racial discrimination. In the 1980s several bishops who were appointed under Mrs Thatcher criticised her government's policy of reducing income tax, particularly on higher incomes, while at the same time not spending more on health, the social services and education.

The Church has always produced and tolerated both dullness and eccentricity. Within its breadth there have been divisions. In the mid-nineteenth century a vigorous new evangelical movement arose within the Church, tilting sharply in the Protestant direction. Soon afterwards a group of Oxford dons tried to recall the Church to the more Catholic elements of its origins. This group came to be called the Oxford Movement, then, colloquially, by the old term 'high-church', as against the 'low-church' evangelicals. By the 1970s the groups seemed to be rather less distinct than they had been. Outside big towns most churches were not obviously high or low. A modern form of service had been introduced to be used instead of the 1662 revision of the Book of Common Prayer. But the revised version is full of alternatives to suit different preferences. Some churches still use the 1662 book once a month, thus placating those who regret the loss of the old language.

In the 1970s a division arose over the proposal that the Church should at last ordain women as priests. Some other churches in the Anglican communion, notably the Episcopalians in the United States, began to do so. By the 1980s the majority of bishops, ordinary clergy and laity appeared to be in favour, and there seemed to be a prospect that a definite positive decision would be made in the 1990s, first by an adequate majority in the Synod, then by Parliament. But some of the opponents were so strongly opposed that there was a possibility of actual schism. The Archbishops of Canterbury and York were criticised for being too much concerned with the avoidance of division, rather than with giving vigorous and inspiring leadership.

For several decades it has been easy to criticise the Church of England both for its links with the establishment and for its own internal rivalries. By the 1980s it was suffering more from indifference than from criticism. Neighbouring parishes have been amalgamated, for lack of clergy – and though the number of clergymen has declined there is too little money to support even the reduced number.

Protestants not belonging to the Church of England were excluded from many offices and places, including the House of Commons, until the early nineteenth century; in those days they were called 'dissenters', but later the rather more polite term 'nonconformist' came to be used instead. Today the term 'members of the Free Churches' is more usual. Of the old dissenting sects, the Baptists and the United Reform Church (consisting of the Congregational and Presbyterian Churches which merged in 1972), are perhaps the most important, though many Presbyterians in England are in fact Scottish people who have taken their own religion southwards across the border. The Quakers have always been a very small and select

156

group, and have their meeting houses, for the most part, only in large towns, but they are immensely respected and in general rather wealthy.

More important numerically than any of these old sects are the Methodists, who follow the movement started by John Wesley in the eighteenth century. He was ordained as a clergyman of the Church of England in 1725, and taught and preached at Oxford for some years, becoming the central figure in a small group who were called 'Methodists' and tried to live a deeply religious life together. Wesley and his followers were religious enthusiasts. They had no objection to the doctrine of the Church of England, but found it indifferent to its Christian duties and to the needs of the ordinary people. It was also indifferent or hostile to Wesley. He travelled over the country preaching, often in the open air, and soon had an immense following. In time many Methodist churches were built and regular preachers and ministers were appointed. The evangelical revival in the Church of England was a belated response to the needs which Wesley had seen earlier, but by then Methodism had already become very important and is probably now the main religion of the people in many northern mining and industrial areas and also in Wales, though the Welsh form is distinct from the English. English Methodists have a regular form of church service and make much use of lay preachers. One great follower of Wesley's path was William Booth, founder of the Salvation Army. Its brass bands play hymn tunes in the streets on Sundays, and its officers do admirable social work.

The Roman Catholic Church was persecuted and weak in England for a long time after the Reformation. Its English hierarchy was extinct from the sixteenth century until 1850, but now England and Wales have four archbishops and fourteen bishops. Many of the Roman Catholics in England are the descendants of immigrants from Ireland, which has always remained predominantly Roman Catholic, and it is sometimes said that Roman Catholic priests are among the main Irish exports to England.

There is no 'Christian' political party and no anti-religious or anti-clerical party either. On the whole Conservatism and adherence to the Church of England tend to go together, though many Anglicans vote against the Conservatives and many members of other denominations vote for them. But the Conservatives regard themselves as a 'national' party, and the Church of England has a special attraction for them because it is identified with the nation. Both nineteenth-century liberalism and modern socialism have their roots partly in nonconformist Protestantism. Among Labour Members of Parliament, there are many who had their first experience of public speaking and of social leadership in their local Methodist churches and church activities. While the intellectual element among Labour Party politicians is perhaps mainly agnostic, many of the working men who have come up through the trade unions are Free Church Protestants. Among Roman Catholic congregations, particularly in the big cities, there are large numbers of Labour Party supporters, though there are also some English Catholics who are to be counted as among the most right-wing of Conservatives.

There are still laws in force restricting trade and some forms of spectator sports on Sundays. By now these laws are uncertain and confused, in some respects absurd, and not regularly enforced. In 1985 the Thatcher government introduced a bill to clarify the legal position and to abolish some of the restrictions on Sunday trading, but it was defeated in the House of Commons, with many Conservatives disobeying their party whips. The Government had no anti-clerical or secularist purpose in introducing this bill. It was trying to replace an absurd and derided law with one which would be respected and enforced.

The statistics of church membership in the official annual *Social Trends* show that all the churches mentioned up to this point lost at least a tenth of their membership in the ten years up to 1988. Also, the number of priests or ministers declined by at least the same proportion. The membership of the main Free Churches has fallen by half in the past forty years, and the decline is still continuing. Even with the Roman Catholic church, which had previously been growing, there was a big loss of active membership. Even so, the Catholic Church has more active members than the Church of England, and more than all the nonconformist Protestant churches. Surveys of actual church attendance show that on an average Sunday about 3 per cent of the population go to Anglican churches, less than 2 per cent to nonconformist churches, and 4–5 per cent to Catholic churches.

The Church of Scotland has been more successful in Scotland than the Anglican Church in England in maintaining a fairly large active membership, amounting to a fifth of the adult population. In so far as Scottish people are concerned with their national identity, the Church of Scotland can be seen as an expression of it. Even so, its membership has been declining at about the same rate as that of the Anglican Church in England.

About three-fifths of all English people, if asked their religion, would probably say 'Church of England', though very many of these never go to church except for funerals and weddings. About half of all marriages are in churches, most of them Anglican. Most people form their own opinions about controversial moral issues. One survey of people's opinions showed that four-fifths of a sample agreed that a pregnant woman should in principle be free to choose to have an abortion – including two-thirds of the Catholics in the sample. In 1986, when 500 children in two secondary schools were asked if they believed in God, half were sceptical, and less than a third found any meaning in religion.

The Methodist, Presbyterian, Reformed and Baptist denominations, together with the national English and Scottish churches, are together approximately similar to what Americans commonly call 'mainline Protestants'. They are all declining in active membership, and account for most of the people who are partially lapsed but not atheist.

Meanwhile, some newer Protestant sects outside the main churches are attracting enthusiastic followers. Several are American in origin. Some of these sects or groups flourish and grow, others decline in their own local environments, depending heavily on the personalities of individual preachers. The combined membership of these 'other Protestant' groups remained unchanged in 1975–85, and in 1985 they had together more adherents than the Methodists. Some of them make severe demands on their adherents, such as abstention from politics or, in one case, from consorting with unbelievers.

The Jewish community is declining. Since World War II and its aftermath few Jews have come to live in Britain; more have left or married non-Jews or abandoned their religion. Some synagogues are rigidly orthodox, some liberal, with their loyal worshippers as well as their less regular adherents. In 1988 the Chief Rabbi was given a peerage on the Prime Minister's recommendation.

Among the religions brought to Britain (mainly England) by people who have come from Asia, Buddhism has had an attraction for some of the native British. Although there are large numbers of Hindus, strict adherence to some Hindu practices seems not to be widespread. Many Sikhs maintain their distinctness more strictly.

There are now nearly a million Muslims in Britain, and the number is increasing. The biggest and grandest new religious building of the 1970s is the London Mosque, by the edge of Regent's Park. Many Muslim leaders are active in maintaining the distinctness of Islam, and numerous Muslim schools have been brought into the state educational system, on a basis similar to that of Catholic schools.

Television and radio give time for broadcasts of religious services, carefully distributed according to supposed demand. Some of these are ecumenical; great occasions like the marriage of the Prince of Wales, and the visit of Pope John Paul II, have lately involved participation of several religious groups, watched with enthusiasm on television by many people. But almost all regular religious life goes on in a local context, not much concerned about the dividing lines between religious bodies.

159

Questions

TABLE 12.1

Religion

	Percentage of Population			Percentage of 'adherents' (Column C) saying 'Yes' to abortion
	Attending a church on a Sunday	Officially recognised members	Stating adherence to	
	A	B	C	D
Roman Catholic	4	5	12	67
Church of England	2	4	58	86
Other Christian (almost all Protestant)	3	5	15	74
Non-Christian religions	n.a.	5	2*	74*
No religion	n.a.	n.a.	10	85
Don't know or no answer	n.a.	n.a.	3	35

The first column shows the approximate proportion of the whole population who actually went to church on one selected non-festive Sunday. The second column B is taken from reports by churches, summarised in the Government's annual publication *Social Trends*. However, each church uses its own criteria for identifying its members.

Columns C and D are derived from a sample survey, carried out by a polling organisation (Marplan) in 1988 for the Abortion Law Reform Society; 1,552 people in 103 parliamentary constituencies were asked to state their religious adherence (if any), and also asked 'Do you think that women should have the right to choose an abortion in the first few months of pregnancy?' *The 'non-Christian' figures should be treated with caution, particularly the 74 per cent pro-abortion. The sample included only a few Muslims, and they were mainly against abortion.

1 How far do the figures suggest that the Church of England is the 'national' church in England?
2 What evidence is there here to support the view that Britain is a Christian country?

The Independent newspaper, on 23 January 1989, summarised the findings of the Rev. Dr Leslie Francis, who put questions to 500 children aged 11–16 in two schools in eastern England at four-yearly intervals from 1974 to 1986.

TABLE 12.2

Changes in young people's religious attitudes		
	1974 %	1986 %
Sceptical about existence of God	36	50
Think church services boring	39	56
Feel God helps their personal lives	42	27

3 During these twelve years many church services were developed in ways to make them more interesting to children. How successful were they?

A large selection of newspapers and magazines is available at any newsagent's.

13

The Press, Radio and Television

1 National Daily and Sunday Papers

The British buy more newspapers than any other people except the Swedes and the Japanese. The daily press differs in two obvious ways from that of any similar Western European country. First, all over Britain most people read 'national' papers, based in London, which altogether sell more copies than all the eighty-odd provincial papers combined. Second, there is a striking difference between the five 'quality' papers and the six mass-circulation popular 'tabloids'.

These characteristics are still more salient with the Sunday press. Almost no papers at all are published in Britain on Sundays except 'national' ones: six 'popular' and five 'quality', based in London. Three appear on Sundays only; the others are associated with dailies which have the same names but different editors, journalists and layouts. The 'quality' Sunday papers devote large sections to literature and the arts. They have colour supplements and are in many ways more like magazines than newspapers. They supply quite different worlds of taste and interest from the 'popular' papers.

Scotland has two important 'quality' papers, *The Scotsman* in Edinburgh and the *Glasgow Herald*. The Glasgow *Daily Record* and *Dundee Courier and Advertiser* survive as 'popular' papers. On Sundays the *Sunday Post*, of Dundee, claims to be read by four-fifths of the Scottish population. Scotland's cultural distinctness is reflected in its press.

The dominance of the national press reflects the weakness of regional identity among the English. The gap in quality is not so much between Labour and Conservative, as between levels of ability to read and appreciate serious news presented seriously. Of the five quality morning papers only *The Daily Telegraph* is solidly Conservative; nearly all its readers are Conservatives. *The Times* and *Financial Times* have a big minority of non-Conservative readers. Of the popular papers only the *Daily Mirror* regularly supports Labour. Plenty of Labour voters read popular papers with Conservative inclinations, but do not change their political opinion because of what they have read. Some of them are interested only in the human interest stories and in sport, and may well hardly notice the reporting of political and economic affairs.

Most of the significant regional newspapers are 'evening' papers, each publishing about four editions between about midday and 5 p.m. London like every other important town has one. All these 'evening' papers are semi-popular, but none has a circulation approaching that of any popular national paper.

Except in central London there are very few newspaper kiosks in town streets. This may be because most pavements are too narrow to have room for them. In towns the local evening papers are sold by elderly men and women who stand for many hours, stamping their feet to keep warm. Otherwise, newspapers can be bought in shops or delivered to homes by boys and girls who want to earn money by doing 'paper-rounds'.

Most of the newspapers are owned by big companies, some of which have vast interests in other things, ranging from travel agencies to Canadian forests. Some have been dominated by strong individuals. The greatest of the press 'barons' have not been British in origin, but have come to Britain from Canada, Australia or Czechoslovakia. The most influential innovator of modern times is partly Indian, and spent his early years in India. He pioneered the introduction of new technology in printing. By now the press in general has replaced expensive old printing methods by new processes which make it possible to operate economically. But it took years of strikes, disrupted production and some violent confrontations before the changes were introduced.

Among the 'quality' papers the strongly Conservative *Daily Telegraph* sells more than twice as many copies as any of the others. It costs less to buy and its reporting of events is very thorough. The *Financial Times* has a narrower appeal, but is not narrowly restricted to business news. *The Guardian* has an old liberal tradition, and is in general a paper of the Left.

The most famous of all British newspapers is *The Times*. It is not now, and has never been, an organ of the government, and has no link with any party. In 1981 it and *The Sunday Times* were taken over by the international press company of the Australian Rupert Murdoch, which also owns two of the most 'popular' of the national papers. Its editorial independence is protected by a supervisory body, but in the 1980s it has on the whole been sympathetic to the Conservative government. The published letters to the editor have often been influential, and some lead to prolonged discussion in further letters. Under the Murdoch régime it has continued a movement away from its old austerity.

Since 1986 *The Times* has had a serious new rival, of similar quality and character: *The Independent*. It has achieved a circulation not much smaller than that of *The Times* – and greater than *The Times*' circulation a few years ago.

The popular newspapers are now commonly called 'tabloids', a word first used for pharmaceutical substances compressed into pills. The tabloid papers compress the news, and are printed on small sheets of paper. They use enormous headlines for the leading items of each day, which are one day political, one day to do with crime, one day sport, one day some odd happening. They have their pages of political report and comment, short, often over-simplified but vigorously written and (nowadays) generally responsible. They thrive on sensational stories and excitement.

The two archetypal popular papers, the *Daily Mail* and *Daily Express*, were both built up by individual tycoons in the early twentieth century. Both had a feeling for the taste of a newly-literate public: if a man bites a dog, that's news. The *Daily Express* was built up by a man born in Canada. He became a great man in the land, a close friend and associate of Winston Churchill, and a powerful minister in his War Cabinet. The circulation of the *Daily Express* at one time exceeded four million copies a day. Now the first Lord Beaverbrook is dead, and the daily sales are not much more than half of their highest figure. The history of the *Daily Mail*, with its more conventional conservatism, is not greatly different.

In popular journalism the *Daily Mirror* became a serious rival of the *Express* and *Mail* in the 1940s. It was always tabloid, and always devoted more space to pictures than to text. It was also a pioneer with strip cartoons. During the Second World War it was the Government's fiercest and most effective critic, and at one time Churchill was tempted to use the Government's special wartime powers to suppress it, but he left it free. After 1945 it regularly supported the Labour Party. It soon outdid the *Daily Express* in size of headlines, short sentences and exploitation of excitement. It also became the biggest-selling daily newspaper. For many years its sales were above four million; sometimes well above.

Until the 1960s the old *Daily Herald* was an important daily paper reflecting the views of the trade unions and the Labour Party. Then it went through several changes, until in the 1970s its successor, *The Sun*, was taken over by Mr Murdoch's company. In its new tabloid form it became a right-wing rival to the *Daily Mirror*, with huge headlines and some nudity. In the 1980s its sales reached four million and exceeded the

Daily Mirror's. Mr Murdoch's News International already owned *The News of the World*, a Sunday paper which has continued to give special emphasis to scandals. But by 1990 its sales were only two-thirds of their former highest figure of eight million.

For a very long time the press has been free from any governmental interference. There has been no censorship, no subsidy. But for several decades it has seemed that some newspapers have abused their freedom. In competing with one another to get stories to satisfy a public taste for scandal, reporters and photographers have been tempted to harass individuals who have for one reason or another been involved, directly or indirectly, in events which could excite public curiosity. Prominent people of all kinds, as well as obscure people who come into the news as victims of crimes or accidents, have been pursued into their homes for photographs and interviews.

In 1953 the organisations of the press themselves created a body called the Press Council, whose main tasks were to defend the freedom of the press and to give its opinions about complaints. Its edicts often criticized the behaviour of some newspapers and their journalists, but were treated with indifference. In 1990 the government asked a committee to examine the situation, and its report concluded that the Press Council had been ineffectual. The organisations of the press appointed a working party of editors to draw up a published code of practice, and a new Press Complaints Commission to enforce it. Journalists should not try to obtain information by subterfuge, intimidation or harassment, or photograph individuals without their consent.

'Intrusions and inquiries into an individual's private life without his or her consent are not generally acceptable and publication can be justified only when in the public interest.' The justification of 'public interest' could include detecting or exposing crime . . . or seriously anti-social conduct, protecting public health or safety, or preventing the public from being misled by someone's statement.

A retired professor of social institutions, who had already been for ten years chairman of the Advertising Standards Authority, was appointed as the first chairman of the Press Complaints Commission. The government had made it clear, with the agreement of the opposition, that this must be the last chance for the press to regulate itself. As the chairman said, in an interview with *The Independent*, reported in the *Sunday Times*, 'It would require only one word from us that the press was not giving its full commitment to enforcing its code . . . and statutory intervention would be on the cards again.'

2 Local and Regional Papers

Local morning papers have suffered from the universal penetration of the London-based national press. Less than twenty survive in the whole of England, and their combined circulation is much less than that of *The Sun* alone. Among local daily papers those published in the evenings are much more important. Each of about seventy towns has one, selling only within a radius of 50 to 100 kilometres. The two London evening papers, the *News* and *Standard*, together sold two million copies in 1980, but they could not both survive, and merged into one, now called *The London Evening Standard*.

Most local daily papers belong to one or other of the big press empires, which leave their local editors to decide editorial policy. Mostly they try to avoid any appearance of regular partisanship, giving equal weight to each major political party. They give heavy weight to local news and defend local interests and local industries.

The total circulation of all the provincial daily newspapers, morning and evening together, is around eight million: about half as great as that of the national papers. In spite of this, some provincial papers are quite prosperous. They do not need their own foreign correspondents; they receive massive local advertising, particularly about things for sale.

The truly local papers are weekly. They are not taken very seriously, being mostly bought for the useful information contained in their advertisements. But for a foreign visitor wishing to learn something of the flavour of a local community, the weekly local paper can be useful. Some of these papers are now given away, not sold but supported by the advertising.

3 The Weekly and Periodical Press

Good English writing is often to be found in the weekly political and literary journals, all based in London, all with nationwide circulations in the tens of thousands. *The Economist*, founded in 1841, probably has no equal anywhere. It has a coloured cover and a few photographs inside, so that it looks like *Time* and *Newsweek*, *Der Spiegel* and *l'Express*, but its reports have more depth and breadth than any of these. It covers world affairs, and even its American section is more informative about America than its American equivalents. Although by no means 'popular', it is vigorous in its comments, and deserves the respect in which it is generally held. The *New Statesman* and *Spectator* are weekly journals of opinion, one left, one right. They regularly contain well-written articles, often

167

politically slanted. Both devote nearly half their space to literature and the arts. The *New Statesman* absorbed *New Society* in 1988.

The Times has three weekly 'Supplements', all published and sold separately. The *Literary Supplement* is devoted almost entirely to book reviews, and covers all kinds of new literature. It makes good use of academic contributors, and has at last, unlike *The Economist*, abandoned its old tradition of anonymous reviews. *The Times Educational* and *Higher Education Supplements* are obviously specialist, and useful sources for any serious student of these fields of interest. *New Scientist*, published by the company which owns the *Daily Mirror*, has good and serious articles about scientific research, often written by academics yet useful for the general reader.

One old British institution, the satirical weekly *Punch*, survives, more abrasive than in an earlier generation yet finding it hard to keep the place it once had in a more secure social system. Its attraction, particularly for the intellectual youth, has been surpassed by a new rival, *Private Eye*, founded in 1962 by people who, not long before, had run a pupils' magazine in Shrewsbury School. Its scandalous material is admirably written on atrocious paper and its circulation rivals that of *The Economist*.

Glossy weekly or monthly illustrated magazines cater either for women or for any of a thousand special interests. Almost all are based in London, with national circulations, and the women's magazines sell millions of copies. These, along with commercial television, are the great educators of demand for the new and better goods offered by the modern consumer society. In any big newsagent's shop the long rows of brightly covered magazines seem to go on for ever; beyond the large variety of appeals to women and teenage girls come those concerned with yachting, tennis, model railways, gardening and cars. For every activity there is a magazine, supported mainly by its advertisers, and from time to time the police bring a pile of pornographic magazines to local magistrates, who have the difficult task of deciding whether they are sufficiently offensive to be banned.

These specialist magazines are not cheap. They live off an infinite variety of taste, curiosity and interest. Their production, week by week and month by month, represents a fabulous amount of effort and of felled trees. Television has not killed the desire to read.

4   Radio and Television

Since the 1970s 98 per cent of British households have had television sets able to receive four channels, two put out by the BBC (British

Broadcasting Corporation), two by commercial companies. Commercial satellite and cable TV began to grow significantly in 1989–90, and by 1991 the two main companies operating in Britain had joined together as British Sky Broadcasting. By 1991 about one household in ten had the equipment to receive this material.

Every household with TV must by law pay for a licence, which costs about the same for a year as a popular newspaper every day. A few people, including those with non-colour TV, pay less. The payments are mainly a compulsory subscription to the BBC, which derives nearly all of its funds from this source, supplemented by any profits that it makes from its weekly programme magazine, *Radio Times*, and from selling some of its productions to other countries.

Unlike the press, mass broadcasting has been subject to some state control from its early days. One agreed purpose has been to ensure that news, comment and discussion should be balanced and impartial, free of influence by government or advertisers. From 1926 first radio, then TV as well, were entrusted to the BBC, which still has a board of governors appointed by the government. The BBC's monopoly was ended in 1954, when an independent board was appointed by the Home Secretary to give licences to broadcast ('franchises') to commercial TV companies financed by advertising, and called in general independent television (ITV). These franchises have been given only for a few years at a time, then renewed, subject to various conditions.

In 1990 Parliament passed a long and complex new Broadcasting Act which made big changes in the arrangements for commercial TV and radio. The old Independent Broadcasting Authority, which had given franchises to the existing TV and radio companies, was abolished. In its place, for TV alone, a new Independent Television Commission was set up in 1991, with the task of awarding future franchises, early in the 1990s, either to the existing companies or to new rivals which were prepared to pay a higher price. The Commission also took over responsibility for licensing cable programme services, including those satellite TV channels which are carried on cable networks. The new law did not change the status of the BBC, but it did have the purpose of increasing competition, both among broadcasters and among producers. It envisaged that a new commercial TV channel, TV5, would start in the early 1990s.

The general nature of the four TV channels functioning in 1991, seems likely to continue, with BBC1 and ITV (soon to be called Channel 3) producing a broadly similar mixture of programmes in competition with each other. ITV (Channel 3) has a complex structure. Its main news is run by one company, Independent Television News (ITN), its early morning

TV-a.m. by another. There are about a dozen regional companies which broadcast in their regions for most of each day, with up to ten minutes of advertisements in each hour, between programmes or as interruptions at intervals of twenty or thirty minutes. These regional companies produce some programmes of local interest and some which they sell to other regions, so that for much of each day the same material is put out all through the country. Some of BBC1's programmes are similarly produced by its regional stations. BBC2 and the independent Channel 4 (which has its own company) are both used partly for special interest programmes and for such things as complete operas.

By international standards it could reasonably be claimed that the four regular channels together provide an above-average service, with the balance giving something to please most tastes and preferences. Some quiz-shows and 'soap operas', or long-running sagas, attract large numbers of viewers – and to some extent the BBC competes for success in this respect. But minority preferences are not overlooked. In Wales there are Welsh-language programmes for the few who want them. There are foreign language lessons for the general public, as well as the special programmes for schools and the Open University. BBC news has always kept a reputation for objectivity, and the independent news service is of similar quality.

Television is probably the most important single factor in the continuous contest for the public's favour between the political parties. Parties and candidates cannot buy advertising time. At intervals each channel provides time for each of the three main political parties for party-political broadcasts, and during an election campaign a great deal of time is provided for the parties' election broadcasts, always on an equal basis. Minor parties get time, based partly on the number of their candidates. In Wales and Scotland the nationalist parties get TV time on the same basis as the three others. Studios and transmitters must be provided free of charge. But often a party prefers to film a broadcast outside the studio at its own expense, for greater impact.

BBC TV Europe broadcasts some of its own programmes by satellite, and from 1991 BBC TV International began to sell and distribute its World Service TV news in English and some other languages.

The BBC's Radio 4 is the main general interest radio service, with some items run by regional studios. Radio 3 is for minority interests, including music, '2' for light entertainment, '1' for pop music and '5' for sport, education and children's programmes. There are also several dozen local BBC radio stations, covering the whole country. The world wide radio service has been established for a long time, and is the only activity of the BBC to receive a government subsidy.

The BBC runs several dozens of local radio stations, which compete with independent commercial rivals, financed by advertisements. All provide a mixture of local news and comment, with some entertainment matter, mainly pop music, in between. In 1991 the Home Secretary appointed a new Radio Authority to take over the functions related to radio of the old IBA, and in particular to grant new licences to broadcast. In the 1990s there should be one or more new commercial radio stations broadcasting nationwide, including one 'non-pop' station, possibly for continuous broadcasts of classical music.

The law of 1990 leaves the Home Secretary with a general responsibility for radio and TV, and he appoints two independent bodies to act as safeguards against abuse. If anyone thinks that there has been unjust or unfair treatment, or unwarranted infringements of privacy, in any radio or TV programme, he or she may bring a complaint to the Broadcasting Complaints Commission whose members are appointed by the Home Secretary.

The second body, the Broadcasting Standards Council, was given a statutory basis by the law of 1990. Its establishment was in part a response to a Clean Up TV pressure group, inspired mainly by a retired school teacher, Mrs Mary Whitehouse, whose vigorous campaigning had made her a well-known personality, often invited to appear on TV herself. This Council has to consider the portrayal of sex and of violence, and matters of taste and decency, in any radio or TV programme or advertisement; to draw up a code of practice; to consider complaints, monitor programmes and undertake relevant research.

Questions

TABLE 13.1

Sales of national newspapers, December 1990
(thousands)

	Daily		Sunday	
Quality	The Times	410	The Sunday Times	1,152
	The Guardian	425	—	
	The Independent	406	Independent on Sunday	380
	Daily Telegraph	1,064	Sunday Telegraph	588
	Financial Times	289	The Observer	561
Middle popular	Daily Express	1,536	Sunday Express	1,627
	Daily Mail	1,694	Mail on Sunday	1,848
	Today	510		
Mass popular	The Sun	3,675	News of the World	4,834
	Daily Mirror	2,962	Sunday Mirror	2,770
	The Star	848	Sunday People	2,448
			Sunday Sport	355

TABLE 13.2

Sales of national papers over 30 years
(millions of copies)

	1962	1990	% change
Quality : Daily	2.0	2.6	+30
Quality : Sunday	1.9	2.7	+40
Others : Daily	15.6	10.9	−22
Others : Sunday	21	13.9	−36

1   Can these changes be related to changes in education and the class structure?
    Are the British peculiar in buying so many 'popular' papers?

2   Why do British people buy so few regional morning papers?
    What is the significance of the dominance of the national (London-based) press?

3   What are your views about the possible methods of financing television? Would it be wise to end the compulsory licence fee for support of the BBC?

4   Is it practicable to impose standards of decency and restraint on the media?

Road signs in Wales are in Welsh and English.

Eilean Donan castle in Scotland.

14

Wales, Scotland and Northern Ireland

1 The United Kingdom and its Component Parts

This book is about Britain, but that word has no clear definition. When people say 'Britain' they usually mean the 'United Kingdom of Great Britain and Northern Ireland', which is a single state, and as such a member of the European Community and United Nations. Some people mistakenly call this whole unit 'England', and in doing so annoy the Scots and Welsh. They consider their parts of the island of Great Britain to be distinct 'nations', though they, and the people of dozens of inhabited Scottish offshore islands and Anglesey (or Ynys Mon) off Wales, are wholly within the United Kingdom

Wales and Scotland both have their own internal administrations, each with a Secretary of State who is a member of the UK cabinet – though some services which are separate for Scotland are not separate for Wales. One irksome effect of these arrangements is that some official statistics are produced separately for the four parts of the UK, some put England and Wales together, some refer to Great Britain but not Northern Ireland, and some cover the whole UK.

Scotland and Wales both elect their MPs to the UK House of Commons, by the same electoral system, with each seat won by the candidate who receives more votes than any other. Both have more seats per million people than England has. Scottish and Welsh politicians have been important in the UK's national affairs. Neil Kinnock, who became leader of the Labour Party in 1983, is a Welshman. He represents a Welsh seat in the House of Commons; so too did his two predecessors as leaders of the party. The UK's last Liberal prime minister, Lloyd George (1916–22) was Welsh. In the period 1892–1964 half of the UK's prime ministers were Scotsmen.

In both countries the Labour Party is very strong in the old industrial areas where most of the people live. At every general election since 1959

Labour has had more votes and won more seats than the Conservatives in both countries. But for most of this time the Conservatives have been in power in the UK, and therefore in charge of the internal administrations, with Conservative ministers for Scotland and Wales. On the other hand, at three of the four general elections won by Labour in this period the Conservatives won more seats than Labour in England, so that it was the Scottish and Welsh votes that put Labour into office.

In Scotland support for Labour increased in the 1980s. In 1987 the Conservatives won only ten seats in Scotland, to Labour's fifty (out of seventy-two). The allied parties of the centre won nine seats, the Nationalists three. In Wales Labour won twenty-four of the thirty-eight seats – eight more than in 1983.

Both Scotland and Wales have for a long time had their nationalist parties, with aims ranging up to the extreme of complete independence. These parties gained enough support in the early 1970s to cause alarm in the major parties, particularly Labour. At the October 1974 election the Scottish Nationalists got 30 per cent of the Scottish votes and won eleven of the seventy-one Scottish seats in the House of Commons. As the Labour government in London had only a tiny overall majority (which it soon lost through defeats in by-elections), it needed to take action to identify its party with the ideas which were causing many Scots (and small but increasing numbers of the Welsh) to vote for their Nationalist politicians.

In 1978–79 a bill was passed by Parliament to increase the autonomy of Scotland and Wales within the Kingdom, and to provide for them to elect national parliaments (though still keeping their seats in the UK House of Commons). But some English Labour MPs did not like these privileges, and the bill was finally passed with a requirement for a referendum in each of the two nations. To bring the bill's provisions into effect there must be not only a majority of those voting, but at least 40 per cent of those registered to vote. In Scotland the votes were 32.88 per cent 'Yes' and 30.78 per cent 'No', so the bill collapsed. A similar provision for Wales produced 12 per cent 'Yes' votes and 47 per cent 'No'. So the bill failed. The Scottish Nationalists then moved a vote of no confidence in the Government and the Government was defeated. At the ensuing general election, which returned the Conservatives to power, the Nationalists lost nine of the eleven seats which they had held before. The nationalist momentum had collapsed and did not revive in the next eight years – though the Scottish Nationalists showed signs of a possible recovery in 1987–90.

Northern Ireland is within the UK and most of its people feel themselves to be British, though a minority do not. Their political parties are entirely different from the British, being based on the Protestant and Catholic communities.

The islands of Jersey and Guernsey, near the coast of Normandy, and the Isle of Man (in the Irish Sea) are not within the UK, though all are smaller in area than several Scottish islands, and less far from the British coast than some of them. They are not represented in the UK Parliament, they have their own governments and finances, fix their own taxes, and have their own courts and judicial systems. They are self-governing 'crown dependencies'. Their people regard themselves as British. When necessary the UK government represents their interests in foreign relations and in the European Community. They are very prosperous, and benefit from their peculiar status.

2 Wales

The only big towns in Wales are along the south coast and in the nearby coalmining valleys which run down from the southern hills. Less than half of the Welsh people live in the remaining nine-tenths of the country's area, most of which is mountainous and full of medieval ruined castles. The greatest of these, Caernarvon, in the north, was used, according to tradition, for the investiture of Queen Elizabeth II's eldest son and heir, Prince Charles, as Prince of Wales. There are good castle ruins in the south as well, but the castle in the centre of the nation's capital at Cardiff was rebuilt a hundred years ago. Apart from the old castles, Welsh architecture is not distinctive, though Cardiff has some fine buildings of the early 1900s.

Choral singing is a national art. It is a fine thing to hear the spectators' hymns at a Welsh victory over England at the national game of Rugby football at Cardiff. All the Welsh team are likely to have been chosen from towns within an hour's journey of Cardiff.

Another special Welsh art is an ability to use the English language with imaginative elegance, particularly in speech. The poet Dylan Thomas came from a place near Swansea; so did the actor Richard Burton (whose real name was Jenkins). For a long time eloquence flourished among the preachers in the Baptist and Methodist chapels of the southern mining valleys. Now it is heard more in the trade unions and the Labour Party.

The Welsh language, which is Celtic, has survived in parts of the north and west, more spontaneously than the rather similar Gaelic languages of Scotland, Cornwall and Brittany. At the 1981 census 19 per cent of the whole population claimed that they could speak Welsh, as compared with

29 per cent in 1951. In the past twenty years there has been a serious attempt to revive the language. All over Wales children in the counties' schools are required to spend some time learning Welsh, though many of them do not remember much beyond the correct pronunciation of place names like Troedyrhiw and Cwmrhydyceirw. Anyone can claim a right to speak Welsh in a court of law, or to use it in academic examinations. Many official jobs are reserved for people who have at least some ability to speak Welsh. Public documents and notices are in Welsh and English, and road signposts show place names either in Welsh only or in both Welsh and English spelling. Nobody drives to Cardiff without knowing it by that name, but the signposts also call it Caerdydd.

Welsh nationalism is mainly cultural and linguistic. The national flag, with its fine dragon, is regularly displayed, the Welsh national anthem played and sung. The 800-year-old National Eisteddfodd, a festival of Welsh music and poetry dating from the twelfth century, is held each year with official help. Plaid Cymru, the Welsh National Party, won three of the country's thirty-eight seats at the election of 1987, all in the Welsh-speaking far north-west. But in more than half of the constituencies in Wales its candidates received less than 5 per cent of the votes cast, and so lost their deposits. In Cardiff their support was below 2 per cent.

3   Scotland

Scotland has just over a tenth as many people as England, in an area more than half as big. It was a separate kingdom, with powerful local lairds, until 1603, when its King James VI became King James I of England too. From then onwards the two countries had the same monarch, though the Act of Union was not passed until 1707. This Act incorporated Scotland with England in the United Kingdom, but the Scots kept their own legal system, religion and administration and still keep them now. Thus Scotland has never been united with England in the same way as Wales.

Scottish national consciousness is cultural and sentimental, and not much concerned with language. The Gaelic language, a Celtic form, is still used rather than English among the people of some remote Highland districts, but elsewhere most of the people are not of Celtic origin and would have no possible reason for wanting to introduce the Gaelic language, which would be an entirely foreign tongue. English is spoken all over Scotland with a variety of regional accents, but all of these can be at once recognised as Scottish, with the vowels and consonants pronounced more nearly as written than in standard English or any of the regional accents of England. Also, there are many words and phrases which are

Princes Street, Edinburgh.

peculiar to Scottish use, and this is felt to maintain national distinctness quite enough.

Parts of south-western Scotland are full of thriving farms, favoured by a mild climate. But even in this area most of the land is too high for easy cultivation. Two-thirds of Scotland's people live in the industrial belt which stretches from the picturesque Clyde estuary in the south-west, across the country's narrowest part to the River Forth and Edinburgh, then up the east coast to the great fishing port of Aberdeen, which now also serves as the mainland centre for the North Sea's oil industry.

Glasgow has always rivalled Edinburgh in medicine, scholarship and the arts, and in the age of iron and steel nearby coalmines helped the Clyde to become one of the world's main shipbuilding centres. Glasgow's prosperity in the nineteenth century produced a special and distinguished style of architecture, both in the city's public buildings and in the houses of the old bourgeoisie. Lately, with the near-collapse of Glasgow's old industries, the city has suffered heavy unemployment. But efforts at rehabilitation have had some success. A fine new building, in a suburban park, houses the great art collection bequeathed by the ship owner, Sir William Burrell. The soot has been cleaned off the old buildings. There is a fresh confidence in the air. But Edinburgh, as Scotland's administrative and legal capital, is more prosperous. Its annual festival of music and the arts is truly international, and a worthy celebration of the grandeur of the city's setting. Near its castle, across a deep valley from the famous Princes Street, are some of Britain's finest eighteenth-century streets and squares.

Scottish towns look very different from English ones. Architectural traditions have been quite distinct, with certain styles appearing all over Scotland but not at all in England. In the central areas of towns, where in England nineteenth-century building consisted mostly of long rows of two-storey red brick houses, the Scots built grey four-storey apartment-houses. In the past thirty years Glasgow's notorious smoke-blackened old tenement buildings have mostly been demolished, replaced by modern blocks of flats (including Britain's highest tower blocks). At the census of 1981 more than two-thirds of Glasgow's people were tenants of the local council. The streets of most small towns and country villages have little of the grace of the English eighteenth and early nineteenth centuries. Stone has been the usual building material until very recently, though now brick is often to be seen; in fact Scottish architecture seems to be gradually losing its distinctive character.

The most interesting and beautiful part of Scotland – and of the whole of Britain – is the north and west, or the region commonly called 'the highlands and islands'. Great sea-lochs, or fjords, not unlike those of Norway, alternate with wild and empty hills, and on some of the lochs there are farms which can only be reached by boat. Cone-shaped, boggy mountains of 1,000 to 1,300 metres high, separated by deep valleys, cover the whole inland area as well as parts of some islands. Agriculture is hard and poor. Vast new and dull coniferous forests have been planted on the mountains, helped by government subsidies. They give some employment but spoil the scenery. Shooting and fishing are rich men's sports, pursued mainly on estates belonging to old aristocrats or new tycoons of commerce, some of them English, some foreign. The old small towns and villages have hotels and caravan sites, but the country has not been spoiled by overdevelopment. Aviemore in the Cairngorm region of the Central Highlands is the only big ski resort. Thousands of holidaymakers visit the Highlands in the summer, hoping for good luck with the weather.

Many hydroelectric power stations have been built to make use of some of the vast water resources of the Highlands, and North Sea oil has brought a temporary prosperity to the north-east. Elsewhere communities are kept alive partly by tourists, partly by rich men who have big estates to which they come for shooting and fishing, and partly by the few who, like the writer George Orwell, when he lived on the island of Jura, want to escape from the busy modern world. But since 1960 the Highland population has grown for the first time for a hundred years.

The foundation of Scotland's distinctness from England is partly religious. Calvin's influence at first affected doctrine in England and Scotland alike, but when the English adopted the moderately Protestant system of the Anglican Church the Scots would not follow them. Under the religious leadership of John Knox they fully accepted the Reformation and established their own Presbyterian church, which has survived, with some serious breaches in its own ranks, until the present time.

The Church of Scotland performs the function of a national Church. Its services are relatively well attended, and the annual meetings of its General Assembly are attended by the Queen or the Lord High Commissioner as her representative. Its Moderator, elected annually by the Assembly, has precedence in Scotland over the Prime Minister. He is not a bishop; there are no bishops, no hierarchy. The Queen attends Church of Scotland services when in Scotland, but has no formal position in relation to it. Its sole head is Jesus Christ. Scottish Presbyterianism has a puritan tradition, expressed in the past by doctrinal rigidity and by condemnation of Sabbath-breaking, the theatre, dancing and pleasure-seeking, but these severities have largely disappeared. Sundays in Scotland, once notorious for their austerity, are now about the same as in England. There is a large proportion of Roman Catholics, particularly in Glasgow, and hostility between Catholics and Protestants occasionally produces fights, usually associated with football matches.

Because of the Puritan influence education was for a long time more easily accessible to the people and more democratic than in England. Three hundred years ago nearly every Scottish community had a good school, and for a very long time after that, while most students at Oxford and Cambridge were the sons of rich men amusing themselves, the four universities of Scotland were full of poor students who had no means or inclination to do anything but study. Some became school teachers or ministers of the Church of Scotland, but many others took the road to England to seek their fortunes and to use the abilities which education had developed in them. This process is sometimes called the conquest of England by the Scots, and it has not stopped yet.

Many Scotsmen have gone to England to seek their fortunes, but many others have gone farther from home. It has been estimated that there are over twenty million people of Scottish extraction in North America, Australia and other parts of the world. Two hundred years ago the typical Scotsman, hard-working, serious-minded and economical, was noticeably different from the Englishman of the privileged classes, who tended to admire extravagance and a certain frivolity, and this contrast may have much to do with the development of the Scottish reputation for meanness. Modern Scotsmen may still dislike wasting money, but most visitors to modern Scotland come away with an impression that the people are hospitable and generous.

Scottish law, based on Roman law, remains distinct from English. The Scottish courts are organised quite differently from the English, and the law itself is different – though on some matters legislation affecting Scotland has made the law the same in the two countries. Most cases in Scotland are tried in sheriff courts, which have no exact equivalent in England. Sheriffs and sheriffs-substitute are advocates who have been appointed to judicial posts. They deal with fairly minor criminal cases under summary procedure, sitting without juries or with juries to try more serious cases. A Scottish jury consists of fifteen persons instead of twelve, and is not bound to find a person 'guilty' or 'not guilty'; it may find a charge 'not proven'. The most important cases are tried before courts presided over by judges of the Court of Session, who travel around on circuit. They have the official title of 'Lord', but are not members of the House of Lords.

Education, agriculture, housing, health, planning, roads, transport, public order and local government are the responsibility of departments of the Scottish Office, under the political control of the Secretary of State for Scotland, who must always be a Scottish MP. Legislation concerning these matters has for a long time been separately passed for Scotland. The Scottish health service is based, for example, on the National Health Service (Scotland) Act, and the Local Government (Scotland) Act of 1973 reformed Scottish local government in a way different from the English, with 'regions' instead of 'counties'.

Although Scottish bills are passed by Parliament at Westminster, their details are in practice debated only by MPs representing constituencies in Scotland. (Most, but not all of these, are Scots and some Scottish people represent constituencies in England.) Apart from their work on bills, the MPs for Scotland have for many years held at least six debates a year on aspects of Scottish affairs.

4 Northern Ireland

In a book about Britain something must be said of Irish history in order to make it clear what is the position of Northern Ireland within the United Kingdom. The inhabitants of this large and beautiful island are mainly Celtic in origin, and the majority never accepted the Reformation. In 1801 a new law added Ireland to the United Kingdom. By this time much of the land belonged to Protestant English landlords, and the Act of Union followed a period in which rebellious peasants were brutally repressed. But in the six northern counties the Protestants were not a dominant minority: they were a majority of the population. Most were descended from Scottish and English settlers who had moved into Ireland several generations before. They considered themselves to be Irish but remained as a distinct community, and there was not much intermarriage. There had been conflicts and battles between the two communities, still remembered along with their heroes and martyrs.

The Union of 1801 gave Ireland seats in the UK Parliament, and after the extensions of the franchise in the nineteenth century a nationalist party won most of the seats. Soon its MPs were demanding self-government, or 'home rule' – a status similar to Canada's.

In 1912, when the Liberals were in power with the support of the main group of Irish MPs, the House of Commons passed a Home Rule bill, but it was delayed by the House of Lords. It was bitterly opposed by the Protestant majority of the people in the six northern counties, and by the MPs they had elected. They did not want to be included in a self-governing Ireland dominated by Catholics.

Eventually the island was partitioned. In 1922 the greater part became effectively an independent state, and (in 1949) a republic outside the Commonwealth. (However, the many Irish citizens who live in the UK are not treated as foreigners.) Its laws, on divorce and other matters, reflect the influence of the Catholic Church. Its Protestant population soon fell by half.

The six northern counties remained within the United Kingdom, with seats in the UK parliament, but had their own parliament, prime minister and government responsible for internal affairs.

In the politics of Northern Ireland the main factor has always been the hostility between Protestants and Catholics. On appropriate dates each year both groups commemorate past confrontations with great and bellicose processions. Although some people do not like these sectarian demonstrations, the only political parties which win seats at elections are based on the two communities. The Catholic population has increased;

the Protestants have declined, but are still in the 1990s about three-fifths of the whole.

Until 1972 the Northern Irish Parliament (called Stormont) always had a Protestant majority and a government formed from it. By the 1960s Catholic discontent produced serious riots. The police were mainly Protestants. Their actions against the rioters were seen as partisan. The UK Labour government of the time had sympathy with the Catholics' grievances. The Protestant parties, calling themselves Unionists (that is, supporters of the union of the province with the UK) regularly supported the Conservatives, while some MPs elected for Catholic parties to the UK parliament took little or no part in its business except, in a few cases, to ask for redress of the Catholics' grievances.

In 1969 the UK Labour government sent troops to Northern Ireland, with orders to help impartially to keep order. But to most Catholics UK troops have become identified with the union of Northern Ireland within the UK. Many moderate Catholics dislike the division of the island, but recognise that the union of the North with the Republic could only be imposed against the wishes of the majority in the North, and would probably lead to civil war. Less moderate Catholics have some sympathy with their own extremists, the Irish Republican Army (IRA), who are prepared to use any means, including indiscriminate violence, in support of the demand to be united with the Republic of Ireland.

In 1969–72 the UK governments, first Labour, then Conservative, tried hard to persuade the Protestant politicians to agree to changes which might be acceptable to the Catholics, but made little progress. In 1972 the UK government (then Conservative) decided that the independent regime could not solve its problems, and put an end to it. Since then the internal administration has been run under the responsibility of the UK cabinet. In political terms this decision of Mr Heath's government was an act of self-sacrifice. Until 1972 the Irish (Protestant) Unionist MPs had regularly supported the Conservatives in the UK parliament, but since then they have become an independent group, not united among themselves, and not linked to any UK party: a sort of dissident Protestant nationalist party. Most of them, like the Northern Irish Catholic MPs, members of Sinn Fein, the Republican party, have taken little part in UK affairs except those involving Northern Ireland.

From 1972 onwards successive UK governments have tried to find a 'political solution' to the Northern Irish problems, that is, a solution acceptable to most Catholics and most Protestants. Several devices have been tried, with little or no success. Protestant politicians are elected on programmes which involve refusal to accept compromise. At the

A British soldier in west Belfast walking past a mural supporting Sinn Fein.

A Protestant parade in Northern Ireland.

European Parliament election of 1984, run on proportional representation, that formidable orator the Reverend Ian Paisley got more first preference votes than any other candidate – and in 1988 he shouted insults at Pope John Paul II when he visited the European Parliament at Strasbourg. Mr Paisley was also elected to the UK House of Commons, by a huge majority, in 1987. He has held his seat there since 1970.

Meanwhile the IRA continues its terrorist campaign. It receives both moral and financial support from some descendants of Irish people who emigrated to the United States. Although so many innocent victims have been killed, many of them by chance or through mistakes, it does not seem likely that any different British government policy would have succeeded in preventing the violence that goes on.

Northern Ireland's economy, based partly on farming, partly on the heavy industries of Belfast, has brought its people a standard of living well above that of the Republic, but lower than Great Britain's. With the decline of shipbuilding there is now serious unemployment, and vast sums have been spent by UK governments in attempts to improve the situation.

Questions

TABLE 14.1

General elections in Scotland

	Percentage of votes					Seats				
	1959	1974	1979	1983	1987	1959	1974	1979	1983	1987
Labour	46.7	36.3	41.5	35.1	42.4	38	41	44	41	50
Conservative	47.6	24.7	31.4	28.4	24.0	31	16	22	21	10
Liberal, etc.	4.8	8.3	8.7	24.5	19.2	2	3	3	8	9
Scot. Nat.	2.5	30.4	17.3	11.8	14.0	0	11	2	2	3

Note the decline in support for the Conservative Party.

1 In 1959 the Conservative majority in the UK as a whole was about the same as in 1987. How then has Scotland's political relation with England changed in three decades?

2 How do you account for the rise of support for the Scottish National Party from 1959 until 1974, followed by a collapse (which may well be temporary)? (In 1959, this party had candidates in only 15 of the 71 seats; from 1974 it contested all the seats.)

The 100 metres heats at the Commonwealth Games.

part of Canada was French. (Quebec is still the only part of North America which is mainly French-speaking, and the whole of Canada is officially bilingual.)

The new Commonwealth began in 1947, when India and Pakistan became fully independent. India's membership of the Commonwealth was not affected by its decision three years later to become a republic. All the major colonial territories, in Asia, Africa and the Caribbean, had become independent within twenty years. In every case power was transferred, with the help and agreement of the British government, to ministries responsible to parliaments elected by universal suffrage, but with guarantees of protection for minorities, such as small tribes.

One country at first declared itself independent without British agreement. In 1965 Rhodesia had already enjoyed internal self-government for forty years, but with a regime that in effect gave power to the white minority, who were mainly settlers of British origin. The arrangement was objectionable to other countries in the Commonwealth, and the British insisted that it must be changed. When the leaders of the white-dominated regime unilaterally declared their independence the

British government considered their regime to be illegitimate, and joined the United Nations in imposing sanctions, while refusing to use military force. Eventually the white leaders agreed to an amended system which would give power to a government elected by equal universal suffrage. An election on this basis gave power to black ministers, and the Republic of Zimbabwe was inaugurated in 1980.

In many independent countries of the Commonwealth the British cultural influence survives, and some of their educational systems still reflect this influence. So too with parliamentary and legal processes. Some send military officers to British colleges for training. But British governments, of both parties, have regularly avoided any interference with their relations with other states, or with their internal politics – although in some cases the original institutions have been fundamentally altered, replaced by military rule or other forms of more or less arbitrary power. In the United Nations, members of the Commonwealth are quite often opposed to one another.

In one case a usurping regime was removed, not by Britain but by another country, the United States. The British government was embarrassed in 1984 when United States military forces invaded the Caribbean island of Grenada. The Americans put an end to a revolutionary regime which had taken power by force; they sent its Cuban helpers home, and stayed for a year to ensure the restoration of a constitutional regime, with a free election and a government based on its result. The British complained that the American intervention was improper, but there was soon ample evidence to show that its outcome was welcome to the great majority of Grenada's people, as well as being advantageous to the British.

It is not inconceivable for two Commonwealth countries to make war on one another. There have been hostilities between India and Pakistan, and in 1971 the Indian army helped the people of East Pakistan (or East Bengal) to secede from Pakistan. One outcome of this affair was Pakistan's withdrawal from the Commonwealth, though this withdrawal had no evident effect on its relations with Britain. When the former East Pakistan became the new sovereign state of Bangladesh, it was admitted to the Commonwealth.

Pakistan was the second independent sovereign state to leave the Commonwealth. The first was South Africa, which left in 1961 because other member states had indicated that the policy of racial segregation, or apartheid, was unacceptable.

The Commonwealth has a secretariat, and every year a meeting of heads of government, no longer always in London but circulating among the different member countries. There are also meetings of finance ministers. Meetings are often acrimonious; some leaders of the Third World member states have been inclined to criticise the British. In the 1980s it seemed at times possible that the Commonwealth would break apart over the British government's refusal to support sanctions against South Africa. The British have argued that sanctions would serve no positive purpose, and would be particularly harmful to South Africa's black people.

Meanwhile, members of the British royal family make their visits to member states, and do much to keep alive the symbolic links. In sport there is not only cricket but also the four-yearly Commonwealth Games, which are run on the model of the Olympics and attract a good deal of enthusiasm.

With the few territories which remain dependent Britain has been active in protecting their interests and has had some problems with the neighbouring states. There has been criticism in the United Nations of the continuance of what may appear to be an outdated colonial status. However, the main factor influencing British policy has been the preference of the majority of the inhabitants.

With Hong Kong, Britain's negotiations with China led to a Joint Declaration in 1985, to the effect that, on the expiry of the British lease in 1997, Hong Kong will become a Special Administrative Region of the People's Republic of China, but that its social and economic system will remain unchanged for fifty years.

Gibraltar is geographically a part of Spain, but its people have voted, by a huge majority, in favour of continuing the British connection. After many years of argument there is now at least free movement across the border, and Spanish irritation about Gibraltar seems no longer to be an obstacle to good relations between the two countries.

The most serious difficulties of the 1980s arose over the status of the Falkland Islands, 300 kilometres off the extreme south of Argentina. With an area half the size of Wales, they were first discovered, uninhabited, by British explorers in 1592. A later British expedition gave the islands the name of Falklands. The first settlement was French, from St Malo (hence the other name, 'Malouines', or in Spanish 'Malvinas'). It lasted for three years (1764–67). Soon after this there were brief but unsuccessful attempts at settlement from Britain and from Spain, so small and so far apart that they did not know of each other's presence. In 1833, when the islands had again been deserted for some time, a new settlement from Britain was inaugurated, and it became permanent, with sheep farming as its basis. For a long time the population has been around 2,000, all of British origin.

The islands are 13,000 kilometres from Great Britain, 4,000 kilometres from St Helena, another isolated island in the Atlantic and also a British dependency. The only convenient access is from Argentina. For a long time Argentina has claimed sovereignty over the islands, partly for this reason, and partly on the basis of ancient history, as the successor to the old Spanish claims, which had apparently been abandoned before the Spanish empire ended. The British have tried to find some formula, acceptable to the islanders, which would provide for Argentina and Britain to give joint support to them. But the British and the islanders have refused to recognise the Argentine claim to full sovereignty. When in 1982 a British military force defeated and expelled a much bigger Argentinian army which had invaded the Falkland Islands, the British military action in defending the islanders led to the collapse in Argentina of that country's oppressive military government and its replacement by an elected one.

The success of the military operation, achieved at great cost in spite of the enormous handicap imposed by the remoteness of the place, was helpful to British national morale and self-confidence. It also raised the reputation of Mrs Thatcher, who appeared as an effective leader of a nation united in opposing an act of unprovoked aggression. Although the old empire has almost entirely been dissolved, there is still a sense of duty to those small remaining pieces for which British responsibility continues.

4 Europe

After 1945 British opinion favoured the creation of new European links, and strongly promoted the establishment of the Council of Europe in 1949. But in 1957, when six countries set up the European Community by signing the Treaty of Rome, Britain stayed outside. Concern with Commonwealth relationships, and dislike of common import tariffs and the agricultural policy, were at that time serious obstacles. Later there was France's veto, prompted by De Gaulle's intuitive misgivings, so long as he was President.

By 1970 the British were unhappy at their continuing exclusion. All three parties' election programmes favoured negotiation for entry to the Community. In 1972, after favourable votes in both Houses of Parliament, Britain joined. By this time the Labour Party was divided, the unions and left wing were deeply hostile. The leaders criticised the terms of entry, and the seats allocated to Labour in the European Parliament were left empty.

After Labour returned to power in 1974 the Wilson government solved its problems by holding a nationwide referendum (the first in British history) on the question of continuing membership. A process which the new Government described as a renegotiation of the treaty had by then been completed. Three-fifths of the electorate participated in the vote, with a two-thirds 'yes' majority, so it then seemed that the nation as a whole was solidly committed to Europe. However, this commitment has not prevented British opposition to most attempts to increase the Community's collective powers.

Britain's participation in the European Parliament has shown signs of the awkwardness that De Gaulle had foreseen. When the Community agreed that elections for the Parliament would be held in 1978, with each nation's seats allocated among the parties approximately in proportion to their votes, the British Government left the House of Commons to decide on the British system of election. The elections were delayed for a year. As a result of the vote Northern Ireland has proportional representation for its three seats, but Great Britain has seventy-eight constituencies, each electing its single member by simple majority – the same system as for the national parliament. This system has produced a representation at least as distorted as that in the House of Commons. The 1979 election gave the Conservatives about twenty more seats than their entitlement on a proportionate basis, the 1984 election ten more. In 1989 it was Labour's turn to win ten seats too many. In 1984 the centre Alliance, with a fifth of the votes, won no seats at all, and in 1989 the Green Party had one-seventh of the votes but no seats. Participation in the voting has been between 32 and 37 per cent – much less than in any other country, and much less than in Northern Ireland.

At Strasbourg the leading British party has had many more seats, more privileges and more funds than major French, German or Italian parties with more votes. The British Conservatives formed a separate group, the European Democrats, joined by one Dane and (for a time) by Conservatives from Spain. However, they have had links with others of the centre-right, and most of them have taken a useful and constructive part in the working of the Parliament.

In the matter of decisions by the Council of Ministers, British ministers have often insisted strongly on their own national interest before agreeing to decisions which need to be unanimous, and Britain has opposed the extension of the types of decision for which a majority is sufficient. Mrs Thatcher personally was reluctant to cooperate with the movement towards monetary union and a common European currency. Even with a subject so uncontentious as the health warnings on cigarette packets Britain objected to a standard warning, and to the principle of uniformity imposed upon the individual nations. Similar objections have been made to attempts to develop common social policies. Britain has been slow in implementing resolutions concerning human rights and control of pollution, and has been in more trouble with the European Court than any other country.

Britain's ambivalent attitude to the rest of Europe is well illustrated by the project to join France and England by a railway tunnel under the English Channel. This project is not a European Community venture, but the tunnel will enable passenger and freight trains to run directly between all parts of Britain and the continent (except Spain, where the track-gauge is different). It will also enable cars, lorries and other vehicles to drive from the French motorway near Calais into special ferry trains which will carry them to a terminal near the English coast, linked by motorways to most parts of Great Britain.

The building of the Channel Tunnel was begun in the 1970s, financed by agreement of the French and British governments. But soon the British Conservative government was replaced by a Labour one, and the new Labour government cancelled the project. Building was resumed in 1987, this time financed by private enterprise, and due to be completed by 1993. By that time new railway lines will enable TGV-type passenger trains to run at 300 kilometres an hour from Paris and Brussels to the tunnel, but there will be no new railway on the English side. After going through the tunnel these trains will continue their 110 kilometre journey to London on the existing British railway tracks, already heavily occupied by slow and semi-fast suburban trains which run at average speeds of 50 to 100 kilometres an hour. There is a plan to build a new fast railway route to London, to be completed a few years after the opening of the tunnel.

Unless policy is changed, travellers to Britain will have to put their watches back an hour, with darker evenings and lighter mornings than in France, except possibly for short periods in the spring and autumn.

The time shown on British clocks in the 1980s can perhaps be seen as a symbol of a surviving insular attitude, and even of a nostalgia about Britain's former great-power status. British time in winter is in fact 'correct' time by the sun, which is at its highest point each day at exactly noon over the Greenwich observatory in London. In 1884 an international conference agreed that the world's standard calculations of longitude should be based on the zero line passing through this observatory, as though London were the world's main centre. Greenwich time is not now used elsewhere in Europe.

For periods in the past fifty years, Britain has itself followed Central European time. In 1971 it reverted to its own Greenwich time in winter but has changed to and from summer time at different dates from the rest of Europe. The decision to revert was made by a free vote of the House of Commons (mainly, as with the choice of an electoral system for the European Parliament, by the votes of Conservative MPs). Opinion polls have shown that most people would prefer more daylight in the evenings, at the cost of darker mornings. Traffic studies indicate that the darker evenings produce a net increase in accidents. Business people have complained that, with different hours of starting and finishing work (and going out to lunch), there are fewer hours each day for talks by telephone across the Channel.

The 1990s may well produce a change to a common European time. There is some hope that a new high-speed railway line may be built from London to the Channel Tunnel by 1999, free of customs queues. More generally, there are signs that public opinion favours closer links with Europe: social, economic and political. People like to go to Europe but they do not like passport controls and customs. They do not much like their different clocks. They are embarrassed and ashamed that, for example, fewer British than German people can speak and understand a foreign language well. On every side there is a new desire to know the language of at least one other European country. In the long run it seems inevitable that the British will become more European.

Questions

TABLE 15.1

	Population (millions)	Grade A Staff number	Grade A Staff per million people	1989 election % voting
Luxemburg	0.4	52	120	87
Belgium	10.0	420	42	90
Ireland	3.5	90	27	68
Denmark	5.0	72	14	46
Greece	10.0	139	14	80
Netherlands	15.0	171	12	47
France	55.0	543	10	49
Italy	57.0	354	10	81
West Germany	61.0	553	9	62
Portugal	10.0	90	9	51
Spain	39.0	246	7	55
Britain (UK)	57.0	354	6	36

National origin of European Community Staff

1 Do these small British proportions illustrate something significant about Britain's role in the Community? (Note that Luxemburg, Belgium, Greece and Italy have laws which oblige or encourage people to vote; Ireland had a national election on the same day).

2 Is Britain a 'good' member of the European Community?

3 Assess the importance for Britain of links with the Commonwealth, the United States and the rest of Europe.

4 What do you think about British policy in relation to the Falkland Islands?

5 Do you find it surprising that Britain has a tradition of not having compulsory military service?

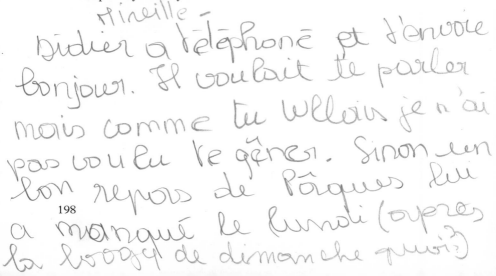